KU-226-202

THE MOBIUS GUIDES

dream interpretation

MICHÈLE SIMMONS
CHRIS McLAUGHLIN

WITHDRAWN FROM STOCK

HODDER

MOBIUS

Copyright © 1994, 2003 by Michèle Simmons and Chris McLaughlin

First published in Great Britain in 2003 by Hodder and Stoughton
A division of Hodder Headline

The right of Michèle Simmons and Chris McLaughlin to be identified as
the Authors of the Work has been asserted by them in accordance with
the Copyright, Designs and Patents Act 1988.

A Mobius paperback

10 9 8 7 6 5 4 3 2 1

All rights reserved. No part of this publication may be reproduced, stored
in a retrieval system, or transmitted, in any form or by any means without
the prior written permission of the publisher, nor be otherwise circulated
in any form of binding or cover other than that in which it is published
and without a similar condition being imposed on the subsequent
purchaser.

A CIP catalogue record for this title is
available from the British Library

ISBN 0 34073477 9

Typeset in Fairfield Light by
Palimpsest Book Production Limited, Polmont, Stirlingshire
Printed and bound in Great Britain by Mackays of Chatham plc,
Chatham, Kent

Hodder and Stoughton
A division of Hodder Headline
338 Euston Road
London NW1 3BH

WITHDRAWN FROM STOCK
3776
3.333
8 2

contents

dream a little dream

At the risk of offending our reader, may we ask a somewhat personal question? Where exactly were you last night?

You may have suddenly found yourself in the middle of a party, not necessarily knowing anyone but still managing to have a pretty good time. Or maybe you were caught up in a battle, desperately trying to escape from the gunfire, aware that your time was running out. . . . Alternatively you may have been having a conversation with an old aunt – nothing very strange about that: unless of course that aunt died years ago. . . . And perhaps you may even have found that with some nocturnal experiences it's not quite so easy to bare all. If you happened to be involved in a rather steamy sexual encounter you could find that even the memory of the night before brings the colour to your cheeks – which is a real give-away to anyone who knows you well!

Now, if any – or even all – of these situations are familiar to you then you've already taken the first step to understanding the world of your dreams. And the more you remember of it, the more you'll begin to understand – which is really what this book is all about: getting the best out of your dreams and helping them to work for you.

Of course, dreams can mean completely different things to different people. Had you been a member of the court of the dissolute Roman Emperor Caligula, for instance, then they may well have been considered prophecies of doom or even signals from the gods themselves. But, if you're a psychologist, dreams are inevitably linked with Sigmund Freud and the deeply buried truths underlying an apparently ordinary 'plot' and cast of characters, as demonstrated in his complex explanation of his own 'Irma Dream'. But you can read more of all this in chapter 3.

On a more contemporary note, if you're a soap addict then a dream can only mean one thing, and the best example is from the hugely popular 70s and 80s American series *Dallas*. To overcome the departures and unplanned returns of the programme's stars, on one occasion *Dallas'* Pam 'dreamt' that husband Bobby had been fatally run over by her sister in front of her very eyes outside Southfork, the family's home. In fact, as far as the producers of the programme were concerned, the 'dream' was convincing enough to last for a whole series!

Whatever dreaming means to you personally, one thing is for sure. Regardless of what you remember in the morning, every night when you go to bed you can be a hundred per cent certain that you will dream. We all do it – and several times every night. And that isn't just hearsay because scientists have proved again and again that REM sleep (the period when we dream) is a crucial part of the sleeping world for all of us.

Making sense of our dreams

However, for the purposes of the waking world, what's interesting is not so much what we dream but what we remember.

A paradox which bedevils all dream research is that most of us remember so little of our dreams. It takes a certain amount of training and practice to hang on to anything more than snippets or overall impressions experienced during the night-time world – most of the time, at least. Yet all of us will wake from time to time with a particularly vivid experience still dominating our thoughts and which stays with us for some time afterwards.

One theory is that we only remember significant dreams – presumably so that we are then able to make some use of them when appropriate. This would certainly explain why there are some days when we wake up and are prepared to swear that not one dream has passed through our mind all night! The fact is that most of our dreams are on the mundane side, full of a rather uninteresting muddle which the memory quite reasonably doesn't bother to store away. Another idea is that dreams act as a sort of sophisticated filing system: sorting what's important amongst all our experiences and dispensing with the rest.

Whatever you choose to believe is the most likely explanation, there can be no doubt that dreams play a role in all of our lives. For proof, just think of how many times you can remember saying, 'I had such a strange dream last night . . .'. A dreamworld is one where events can change abruptly, relatively unknown people can assume unexplained importance, and the absurd seems to know no boundaries. Talking animals, friendships with the Royals, bizarre conversations that defy logic and exotic locations we've never visited before – such can be the stuff of our dreams.

But simply being able to relay our dreams to a friend the morning after fails to exploit the dream to its full potential. Of course dream-telling can be an amusing business – particularly if yours are the type that would only get an 18 certificate from the film censors! But that certainly isn't the full story.

What this book is about is giving you the whole picture: so, telling you how you dream as well as why you dream; what your dreams really are as well as what they mean. We have also included a special personalised directory of your dreams which highlights and explains the most significant dream themes that scientists have, as yet, recorded.

You may feel that the world is hardly in need of another dream book and, admittedly, a cursory glance in most bookshops will reveal a vast array of volumes on the subject – all claiming to give a blow-by-blow breakdown of exactly what your dreams mean. Many operate on the same basis as a dictionary – each word has a specific, unique meaning. It sounds simple enough, and it may even provide a good read, but for dreamers the question is, how useful, or even accurate, can it be?

To start with, the dictionary approach tends to rely on objects as representations of an individual's true feelings. And because our alphabet goes from A to Z, great efforts are made to find objects that can fit into all twenty-six categories – however obscure. Which is why you may find, on the one hand, definitions for dreams that include asparagus (although the people who do actually dream about asparagus must be few and far between!) while on the other hand you get several sentences on the meaning of dreaming about a yodel!

Unfortunately the A to Z format has its limitations, very much in the same way that magazine or newspaper horoscopes divide us all up into twelve neat little packages and then offer an outline of the immediate future based on whichever of the twelve categories we happen to fit into. And while this may be a convenient formula to base the predictions on, in many cases, if the stargazer's prophecies do come true it's more likely to be because the law of averages is on their side, rather than anything else! And the same could be said when it comes to the dream dictionary approach to understanding what happens during our REM sleep. It may be good fun, but the real story is more complex . . . and more fascinating.

In truth, our dreams do not come in neat little packages and do not simply focus on one object, enabling us, on waking, to rush to our dream dictionary so that we can discover the secrets of our true inner selves. It just doesn't work like that.

Firstly, we tend to dream in images and themes rather than of objects. We are also more likely to dream of somebody doing something – whether it is us, someone we know or a complete stranger. Our dreams are like a snapshot, depicting isolated scenes from an event – sometimes the scene is short with very little happening, while at other times we feel our sleeping hours have been action-packed, emotionally as well as physically, leaving us feeling quite drained when we wake up. So, what you dream about is as significant as what you dream of.

Equally important is the state of mind in which you've had the dream. So, you could have a situation where two people reported similar dreams but reacted, within the dream, in completely different ways. Dreaming of an aeroplane may for one person be connected with an impending trip, while for someone who had a pathological fear of heights it would have an altogether different meaning.

Why nothing is what it seems

So, whichever way you look at it – and whatever objects you may look up in that well-thumbed dream dictionary, at the end of the day what's happening in your life, and how you feel about it, is of fundamental importance when it comes to understanding your dreams. In our dream world things are rarely what they seem to be, and dreaming of a fierce gun battle most certainly does not mean that you have a hidden desire to go off and fight in strange lands! However, it could mean that you feel you're being pushed into a decision; or that you're under pressure at work or even that you don't think you'll manage to get all your packing done before you go on holiday. This, as with almost all dreams, could mean a number of things – all depending on who the dreamer is.

This book is concerned with helping you to understand yourself as much as it is about understanding your dreams. For years doctors have recognised the importance of dreams and have actually used dream therapy as a way of treating patients. Admittedly the initial interpretations were somewhat limited and many experts have now revised, if not rejected altogether, some of Freud's original theories on the subject. It's also worth remembering that Freud was a neurologist as well as the world's first psychiatrist, which means that his theories evolved from treating patients who in many cases were deeply troubled. Consequently, it must follow that his dream analysis, and the way he applied it, has its limits for the rest of us.

Ultimately we have tried to make this book as useful, and as accessible, as possible. While not advancing any particular theory, we have tried to offer a practical approach based on some of the current theories that have been put forward by some of the experts in the field. We've included the latest scientific findings about sleep and dreaming, as well as some of the more recent psychological approaches. It would be impossible to offer a definitive guide in a field where there is still so much disagreement among everyone involved, but we hope we've put forward a consensus view on the nature of dreams as well as the art of dreaming itself.

How to use this book

The book is loosely divided into several sections. Chapters 2 to 4 look at the scientific and psychological world of dreams and what people have made of the subject in past times. It is our firm belief that to understand truly what you're dreaming, you need to know why and how. Although theories and articles abound on the hows, whys and whats of dreaming, we have concentrated on tracing a clear path through all the controversy to pick out what is perceived as the present wisdom on the subject.

Chapter 5 looks at how your dreams relate to and reflect your 'real' life, and explains how you can learn to 'read' them.

Of course the whole art of dreaming is an inexact science but, that said, clearly some sources are more credible than others. We have attempted to offer an amalgam of current thought on the subject, trying at all times to provide a practical, as well as fascinating, insight into this much undervalued area.

The third section of the book looks at the whole area of sleep 'problems', as well as children's dreams. We believe that a child's dreamworld demands a chapter to itself – not least because so little has been written on the subject: most of the information concerns clinical data where the subjects have been children undergoing treatment for some kind of psychological disturbance. So, the information is not necessarily relevant to the average healthy child, which is what most of us want to know about most of the time. The importance of understanding childhood dreams is made particularly clear to those parents – which means nearly all parents – who have had to comfort a child who had woken in the middle of the night from a world of threatening monsters and wicked witches: a world that has left the child utterly distraught. Needless to say the child can make little sense of the dream – but chances are, neither can you.

Children's dreams can be very different from ours and the fact that so little has been written on the subject may say something about how much thought our society gives to children. With this in mind, we have tried to make the chapter as practical as possible – to the child as well as the parent: Understanding what your child dreams about and what his experiences mean to him can give you an enormous insight into your child's world – both night and day – which can be both fascinating and helpful in his development.

Within the chapter we have also covered nightmares and night terrors, but recognising that a child's experience is not necessarily the same as a grown-up's, we have included a separate section on nightmares and lucid dreams for adults. This is also designed to explain what is behind these disturbing experiences and suggests how you may be able to take control of the chaotic world of your dreams.

The final section discusses the most common dream themes. We describe the dreams, explain what they mean, how to interpret them in a way that is meaningful for you and then offer you our unique action plan designed to help you to use your dream in a positive and ultimately beneficial way. Rarely are our dreams literal; rather they often consist of images and symbols which have to be interpreted in the light of your own life and preoccupations. Once you learn to understand exactly what they mean, you're well on the road to understanding your dreams.

Dream on

Whatever sort of dreams you have, considering we spend a third of our lives asleep, you can be sure that 50,000 hours of that is spent in your very own dreamworld. To a large extent, it's up to you what you get out of your dreams and it really is a case of the more you put in, the more you get out. There's no denying that some dreams can, at first, seem deeply disturbing. However, once you put them into context and discover what they're really about, they can immediately become more positive – something that can be used constructively.

In fact, you don't need to dream your life away to get the most out of your dreams. Just learn to understand them and how to make the most of them. Then all that's left to do is lie there and enjoy the whole experience. And now turn the page to find out exactly how!

2

the science of dreams

While people have always devoted a lot of time and thought to understanding the significance of dreams and how to react to them, it is only relatively recently that researchers have started investigating exactly what is going on in our minds and bodies while we're dreaming.

The first suggestion that a dream might be the product of our imagination rather than some message from somewhere 'outside' came in the writings of Erasmus Darwin in the late eighteenth century. He commented on the fact that we normally accept the bizarre goings-on without surprise, as though normal judgement is somehow suspended. He also put forward the theory that dreams prevent us from going mad by stopping us having hallucinations – an idea which is still around in a slightly different form today.

Proper scientific study of dreams really only developed during the last half century or so. It was in the 1950s that a group of

American researchers in Chicago identified the so-called REM (Rapid Eye Movement) sleep – periods of relatively shallow sleep in which the eyes flickered about under the closed lids. This finding came as something of a surprise to the original researchers, who had previously thought that people only moved their eyes when awake and looking around. It opened the door to a whole new world of sleep studies, and within a few years further investigation of this new phenomenon enabled scientists to begin systematic research into what happens when we dream.

Interestingly, one of the pioneers of dream research, William Dement of Chicago, stumbled on the connection between eye movements and dreams when he noticed that sleepers woken from REM sleep nearly always said they had been dreaming. At other times, when the eyes were still, subjects couldn't remember any dreams when woken up.

Today, there is still some controversy about whether dreams only occur during REM sleep and not during other stages. However, if any dreaming does occur at other times, it is much less vivid, less dramatic and relatively brief. On the other hand, REM sleep is always associated with dreaming.

Brain power

Scientists are able to find out a lot more about the physical changes associated with all kinds of sleep by wiring their sleepers up to various electrical measuring devices to record changes in their brainwaves, eye movements and muscle tension. Special lighting and the use of video cameras enable the researchers to watch people being studied in the lab while they sleep. Surprisingly, perhaps, people do actually manage to sleep in these researchers' labs, despite having a variety of sensors attached to their head, face and neck and being woken at intervals during the night!

Unfortunately, studying people in labs is an expensive business, says Professor Jacob Empson, Head of Psychology and sleep expert at Hull University, and author of *Sleep and Dreaming* (see page 154). Some studies will involve just one practice night followed by a maximum of two or three actually wired up to the measuring instruments. This doesn't give researchers much time to look at any mid-term or long-term effects – for example sleep deprivation – and limits the sleepers' opportunities to have an interesting variety of dreams for study.

Research has shown that all mammals experience periods of REM sleep – although what their dreams are about and what they mean remains a mystery. Dolphins are thought to sleep with half their brain at a time – the other side (and the other eye) remain alert and watchful for any dangers! Adult humans spend around 15 to 20 per cent of the night's sleep dreaming, while for young babies the proportion is dramatically greater – around 50 to 70 per cent of their sleep is REM sleep.

We tend to think of eight hours a night being the normal amount of sleep, and this is borne out by studies in sleep labs. The vast majority of us take roughly this amount given the chance, although some will need up to an hour more or less. Once we're asleep, however, we all follow the same pattern as far as bouts of REM sleep are concerned, whether we think of ourselves as good or poor sleepers and regardless of whether we remember any dreams.

The stages of sleep

After first falling asleep, we gradually progress into ever deeper sleep, through what scientists call stages 1 to 4, which are determined by measuring brainwaves. The first stage is when we are drifting into sleep, and normally lasts no more than 10 minutes. People woken at this point will tell of disconnected and fantasy-type thoughts, but they are not the powerful visual experiences of a true dream, and there is no evidence of the physical changes which accompany REM sleep.

As we sink deeper into sleep, the brainwaves become deeper

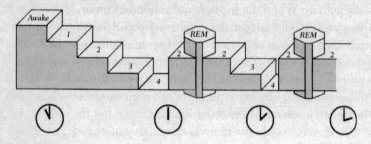

The stages of sleep

and slower, passing through stage 3 until we reach stage 4. At this point, the EEG (or electro-encephalograph, which is measuring the brainwaves) will be showing huge, evenly spaced waves known as delta waves. When we first fall asleep, we spend most of the time in these deeper 3 and 4 stages. It is only after a minimum of 45 minutes – and usually longer – that we have our first session of dreaming sleep. For most of us, this will last up to 15 minutes, after which we slip once more into deeper, non-dreaming stages of sleep.

The proportion of time spent in the various non-dreaming stages will vary from one person to another. There is some evidence that those who seem to need least sleep, and say they can manage on five or six hours a night, spend more time deeply asleep (that is, in stage 4 sleep) than the rest of us. However, we will all have periods of REM sleep every 90 minutes or so throughout the night, and these will generally last up to half an hour at a time. Added up, our dreams last on average for about an hour and a half every night.

There have been many different attempts to explain the purpose of sleep. After all, it is rather odd that we spend up to a third of our lives unaware of the 'real' world, and for early man it must have represented a dangerous period of vulnerability to outside attack.

At one time, scientists believed that some mysterious substance – labelled hypnotoxin – built up in our bodies during daily activity. When the hypnotoxin reached a certain level, they thought, it would trigger the onset of sleep. Unfortunately, no one has ever been able to identify any substance which could be this hypnotoxin. What's more, most existing evidence worked against this theory, not least the fact that we can force ourselves to stay awake for quite long periods if we want to. Others believed that we slept in order to give our brains a rest – but the discovery of REM sleep, when the brain is definitely not at rest, put paid to that idea.

One of the most appealing explanations is that sleep gives our bodies the opportunity for repairing any damage and restoring our 'working parts' to peak condition. While we're asleep, our metabolism slows down, and our immune system can concentrate on fighting any infection or other damage. This process may be helped by the increased production of growth hormone during sleep. From a layman's point of view, this kind of explanation seems to make sense, in that we feel better after a good night's sleep, and rotten if we sleep badly.

The truth is, however, that scientists don't actually know whether this is the true explanation or not. They know sleep is important and that without it we function less well physically and mentally, but so far they don't really know why!

The patterns of sleep

While most normal adults will follow the same sort of sleep pattern each night, all of us will tend to sleep less well as we get older. Interestingly, it tends to be the deeper levels of sleep (stages 3 and 4) that we increasingly miss out on, while the amount of dreaming stays much the same.

With children, however, the picture is very different. In their first year of life, babies alternate between deep and REM sleep with no in-between stages. It is thought that around three-quarters of their sleeping time is spent in REM or 'active' sleep. Unlike adults, they will often go straight into this active phase, rather than having a period of deeper sleep first. By the time they're three or so, they'll have around three hours' REM sleep a night, reducing to the normal adult quantity of about two hours a night by the time they reach the age of ten. As they get older, and learn the difference between night and day, they spend more time awake and move towards the adult pattern of sleep.

However, there does seem to be one blip in this otherwise smooth progression towards adult sleep patterns. As any parent knows, teenagers are often extremely unwilling to get up at a reasonable hour of the morning, and have to be practically dragged out of bed. It may be some comfort to know that there is a certain amount of evidence that adolescents do genuinely need more sleep than adults, and that's even if you allow for their natural tendency to stay up half the night if left to themselves.

The body and sleep

Wiring sleepers up to various electronic measuring devices can tell sleep lab researchers a lot about what happens to our bodies during REM sleep, although interpretation of these findings and their significance is less straightforward. The most obvious sign of REM sleep is the rapid eye movements themselves – observers can see the eyeballs darting about beneath the sleeper's closed eyelids. In addition, the heart rate speeds up, the blood pressure rises, and the pattern of brainwaves measured on the EEG changes from the long, slow 'delta' waves of stage 4 sleep to a more erratic picture.

One rather odd finding is that we lose muscle tone while we're dreaming. What this actually means is that we're almost literally unable to move, which may explain the common dream sensation of being rooted to the spot or struggling unsuccessfully to run from some hazard.

Having developed the ability to identify REM sleep, the Chicago researchers who pioneered scientific sleep studies wanted to find out whether it served any useful purpose. Several experiments were conducted in the lab in which sleepers were wakened as soon as they entered a phase of REM sleep, while another group were woken up the same number of times during other stages of sleep.

After they'd been put through this routine for about a week, the subjects who had been prevented from dreaming seemed to be showing signs of serious psychological stress, while the others were simply tired and irritable – as might be expected. This was taken to mean that dreaming is necessary for our psychological health, and as sometimes happens, this piece of research caught the imagination of the media and was widely publicised. Even now, it is often dragged out as conventional, accepted wisdom that if we don't dream, we go mad.

Unfortunately, other experiments carried out later by Dement in Chicago and others elsewhere failed to show the same effects, and experts now agree that there is no evidence that depriving someone of their dreams leads to psychological disorder. Perhaps the fact that the original theory offered a simple and believable explanation of the mystery of why we dream accounts for its persistence, but it doesn't appear to be true.

Dream recall

What these scientific studies can't tell us, of course, is what the experience of REM feels like from the dreamer's point of view. Although everyone has periods of REM sleep, some people claim that they don't dream. The common sense answer to this paradox is that they do dream but don't remember, and this idea is borne out by sleep lab studies. Researchers have found that when a sleeper is woken during or immediately after a period of REM sleep, they will be able to describe a dream, although some were more detailed and vivid than others.

More differences between 'dreamers' and 'non-dreamers' emerged when they were woken after the period of REM sleep had ended. The people who claimed not to dream were less likely to be able to recall their dreams after a delay, reinforcing the theory that they simply forgot their dreams more easily.

Another study put forward a different and intriguing explanation. The researchers found that, while 'non-dreamers' told of chaotic and strange images when woken from REM sleep, they were prone to say that what they were describing were waking thoughts rather than dreams, despite their bizarre nature.

Judging by EEG measurements, all of us will experience between three and six periods of dreaming in an average night, so even those people who can usually remember a dream on waking in the morning must still have forgotten most of their night's adventures. Some experts believe that when a dream lasts longer than a few minutes, it is only the latter part that will be recalled, the beginning being lost for ever. Since it seems the dreamer must wake during or immediately after a dream to have any chance of recalling it, it may be poor sleepers, most prone to waking several times a night, who remember most. This will be reinforced if they actually switch the light on or get up while the dream is still fresh in their minds.

One experiment in a sleep lab showed that people who were woken during a period of REM sleep and asked to look up a phone number before recording the details of their dream had forgotten most of it before they came to writing it down. By contrast, writing the report immediately they woke meant they could recall much more. As Professor Empson points out, 'If dreams are meant to be messages to ourselves, you would expect them to wake you up, or at least that we would remember more than we do of them.'

All of this suggests that something happens during sleep to impair our ability to remember. Experiments in sleep learning showed that the idea that we could learn something new – such as a foreign language – by playing a cassette while we slept was, unfortunately, completely wrong. Researchers then tried reading out short sentences to people who had just been woken up.

They found that their subjects remembered little or nothing unless brainwave changes on an EEG showed that they were fully awake, and remained awake for a short time afterwards.

By their very nature, dreams tend to be chaotic and illogical, and our inability to impose any rational structure on them may make them even less memorable. Those which do stay in our minds tend to be the more dramatic and colourful, or the ones which we see as having some special significance for us personally. It is an intriguing fact that if you simply ask people what they dream about, they will come up with all manner of fascinating stories, but only about five per cent of people seem able to manage exciting dreams while in a sleep lab. Probably, we only remember a small proportion of our dreams. We are less likely to recall a muddled and rather dull dream – and that's probably what most of them are.

This last fact may explain why some people believe they don't dream in colour. Sleep lab studies, which give the most accurate descriptions because they are reported immediately the sleeper wakes up, suggest that most people do dream in colour, although it can vary from vivid to relatively pale. Otherwise, memories tend to be partial and imprecise, and we recall what seemed to us to be the dominant aspect of our dream, in which the colours involved may have played little or no part. There is some evidence that colour has played a more prominent role since people started seeing films in colour at the cinema. Colour TV and videos have probably increased this tendency still further.

Why we dream

While scientists have now built up an impressive store of knowledge about dreaming, they are much less confident in offering explanations of what it all means. They can state with reasonable certainty that everyone dreams, and for how long, and describe in detail the physical changes involved. It is much more difficult to understand why we regularly enter this mysterious other world and what its purpose is.

Sleep scientists point out that there is a paradox in dreaming which needs to be explained. A person who is deprived of REM sleep will take the opportunity to catch up on what's been missed as soon as he is allowed to sleep without interruption, even when this means having less non-REM sleep. This suggests that it is important in some way, yet virtually all of the dreams we have during REM sleep are forgotten. A lot of effort has gone into finding a way of explaining this peculiar fact, and some scientists have concluded that it must imply that the actual content of our dreams with which we are so fascinated can't be that important after all!

Most of the more recent theories have looked for explanations in terms of what's happening in the sleeping brain. While we are awake, a part of the brain known as the 'hindbrain' collects signals from our senses and transmits them via electrical discharges to the 'cortex' which interprets the signals. During sleep, most of this message transmission is shut down – we don't respond to sound or other external events as we would when awake. Nevertheless, the cortex must continue to 'tick over', and the theories suggest that the hindbrain makes sure this happens by sending random signals which have no connection with any real events to keep the cortex going. According to this view, dreams are the result of the cortex trying to make sense of these meaningless signals as if they were real messages like the ones it normally receives from the external world.

Other theorists have taken this idea further by suggesting that the cortex uses this apparently random activity to dump information which is of no use or relevance to the person's real life. By getting rid of the rubbish, it is argued, we help ourselves to store away the information and experiences which will be useful to us later.

Some support for this theory comes from research in Israel in which volunteers in a sleep lab were shown patterns on a computer screen before going to sleep. Those people who were then allowed to sleep through the night without interruption remembered more of what they'd seen than those who were woken up every time they started on a phase of dreaming sleep. This suggests that REM sleep may play some role in retaining memories, and that being deprived of it disrupts the mechanism in some way, possibly by disturbing the sorting-out process.

Another attempt to explain why so much of our dreaming is forgotten is the 'neural net' theory developed by Graeme Mitchinson and Francis Crick (who won a Nobel prize for his part in the discovery of the molecular structure of DNA). They compared dreaming to a 'cleaning up' mechanism in the brain. According to Crick and Mitchinson, 'We dream to forget'. What is going on while we dream is a kind of reverse learning in which we get rid of useless information while at the same time keeping the cortex functioning. This means that the content of our dreams is simply nonsense information for which we have no use. By getting rid of it in dreams, we prevent our brains from becoming overloaded and leave more room for the stuff we do need.

In the late 1970s, American researchers looked for an explanation in the measurable physical activities going on during sleep, and came up with what the experts call the 'activation-synthesis' hypothesis. They claim that since one of the cortex's main functions is to interpret the outside world, it's reasonable to assume that it will go on doing this with any input it receives that appears to originate there. It makes no difference that the signals it receives during REM sleep are simply chaotic and have no connection with reality because they're generated within the brain itself: it tries to make sense of them just the same.

How we dream

Others have developed this theory still further, using sophisticated analysis of eye movement during dreams which suggests that we experience two different kinds of image. One is the vivid visual hallucination, the other is a less spectacular series of running images which, they claim, constitute the mind's attempt to impose a 'plot' on to the primary images.

It might logically be expected that people who generally have a strong visual sense, and who tend to think in pictures would have more colourful and vivid dreams than those who are more word or speech orientated. In practice, however, research by Professor Empson's team in Hull doesn't support this common sense view. It seems that dreams never live up to our preconceived ideas!

It's plain that many of our normal mental abilities continue to function while we're dreaming. We're still able to count and obey instructions given to us, and even understand or read the foreign languages we know in waking life. We are also still sensitive to certain signals from the outside world, despite the fact that many of us can sleep through loud thunderstorms or even the alarm clock going off. Sometimes, such outside stimuli actually penetrate our consciousness sufficiently to be incorporated into our dreams (for more on this, see chapter 5). Recognising the stimulus in the resulting dream image isn't always easy, however.

One study in the sleep lab at London's University College involved playing recorded information to a person who had just begun a phase of REM sleep. Names in particular seemed to provoke a response – but one man who heard the name Alice didn't associate it with a woman but with the town of Alice Springs in Australia!

It was in the course of studying this odd phenomenon known as incorporation that researchers were able to demonstrate that dreams run in 'real time'. In other words, the events of the dream last as long as they seem to – time is not speeded up or otherwise distorted. In one experiment, dreamers were sprayed with a few drops of water while they were in a REM phase of sleep, then woken a few minutes later. When asked to recount their dream, those who had incorporated the spraying into the plot of their dream did so at exactly the moment it had really happened.

'Dream time' is apparently not telescoped in the way we sometimes imagine. When, for example, we hear the sound of the alarm clock, we may incorporate it into a dream by turning it into the sound of church bells. When we wake up, we convince ourselves that the whole of a fairly complicated dream set in a church took place after the clock had gone off. This is just one of the peculiar tricks of memory we play on ourselves to try and make sense of our chaotic dreams.

Some theorists have suggested that it is only while we're dreaming that the whole of our memory store is available to us at once, and have looked for clues as to how memory works generally by studying the associations formed in dreams. For instance, we've all experienced the situation where we simply cannot remember a person's name – either someone we know personally or a well-known public figure. 'You know, that man on the television who introduces the proms every year, used to be a newsreader, used to have dark hair, going a bit grey,' and so on. For some reason, you simply can't get the name out of your memory, even though you know perfectly well that it's in there somewhere. Then, that night, you dream you're helping a man in a white apron and tall white hat to make bread, and you wake with the name on your lips: 'Of course, Richard Baker!' Another time, you may go to bed with the sound of a particular song going round in your head, only to find you dream of someone you haven't seen or thought about since you were at school, but who used to like that particular song.

Memories are made of this

Occasionally, dreams may give access to memories in a more direct way. Psychologist Christopher Evans has written of an interesting experience of remembering in a dream a fact which he could not bring to mind in his waking state. Having had his watch stolen, he realised when he reported the theft to the police that he could not remember the make, despite having seen it on the watch face thousands of times. He was disappointed because he knew this meant there was virtually no chance of ever getting it back even if it were found. A few nights later, he woke with a vivid dream still in his mind. He'd been looking at a close-up of the watch face in which every detail was visible, including the make: Bifora was clearly spelled out in capital letters before his eyes. Evans deduced that his mind had somehow gained access to the part of his memory where the watch name was stored during the dream, even though he did not consciously know that he remembered it.

As a computer scientist as well as a psychologist, Evans used this experience as the starting point for his 'computer' theory of dreaming: that the mind takes the opportunity of the peace and quiet of sleep, when few signals are coming in from the external world, to sort and refile the experiences of the preceding day. It files away some knowledge for long-term storage, and filters out the unwanted material. According to this theory, the dreams we remember are the result of the conscious mind briefly intercepting this mostly unconscious – and therefore unremembered – process.

Although the scientific studies carried out in sleep labs have produced much interesting and valuable information about dreaming, they have not allowed researchers to state with certainty that they know why we dream and what the purpose is.

According to Professor Jacob Empson, this shouldn't surprise us:

The truth is that we still have no real understanding of what consciousness is. We think we should be able to discover what dreams are for, but they are simply an unusual form of consciousness which is not familiar to us when we are awake. Until we can answer the first question about the function of consciousness, we can't really expect to grasp the purpose of dreams.

While the latest theories are based on scientific observation and fit in with the information collected in sleep labs about what's going on in the brain, they don't account completely for the dreams which people actually experience. Nevertheless, Professor Empson says that a proper explanation of dreams would have to take account of the kind of physiological facts revealed in laboratory studies and also the psychological component of dreaming:

> *The person whose brainwaves are being measured and inter-preted in the sleep lab is the same person when they are awake. It's the same set of brain circuits firing, so the results aren't purely random. In other words, each individual's dreams must relate to their daily preoccupations.*

There's support for this view from Martin Seligman, whose work suggests that, while the content of dreams might seem random or arbitrary, we gain understanding in the process of trying to impose meaning on them.

Unfortunately, years of careful scientific study have still left great gaps in our understanding of why we dream and what our nocturnal experiences may mean. If for example it is true, as some experts believe, that we dream to forget, why should we have recurring dreams? There would be no way they could happen if they were purely and simply a response to random signals or part of the process of memory sorting. Many people would also feel that such prosaic interpretations simply don't explain the kind of dreams they experience or the profound effects such dreams have on their thoughts and emotions. We will look at some possible explanations of these conundrums about the meaning of dreams in the following chapters.

3

the psychology of dreams

Interpreting your dreams would be easy if it were simply a matter of associating a certain image with a particular significance. From the earliest times, and certainly today, people have always believed that understanding dreams requires quite a lot of effort from either dreamer or analyst – or sometimes both. The true message is wrapped up in confusing images and symbols from which the meaning must somehow be extracted (see chapter 8). Despite this personal element, you only have to discuss your dreams with other people to realise that individuals' dreams have a surprising amount in common.

Nevertheless, research has shown that people from completely different cultural backgrounds tend to share a similar dream repertoire. In fact, according to the experts, most people will at some time dream of falling, or of being pursued and unable to get away because they can't move, to take some of the most common examples. The meaning placed upon these dreams, however, is likely to vary from one individual to another.

This simple truth was recognised by the earliest known inter-preter of dreams, Artemidorus. He was born in the second century AD in Ephesus, Asia Minor, and the five volumes which make up his 'Book of Dreams' were regarded as the best guide to the subject until Freud came along some 1,700 years later. Artemidorus said:

The same dream does not always have the same meaning in each case and for each person. It can vary depending on the time and place, and it can vary in length and content. In particular, if we wish to interpret a dream correctly, we need to take note of whether the person dreaming it is male or female, healthy or sick, a free man or a slave, rich or poor, young or old.

The influence of Freud

In this, Artemidorus was rather more wide-ranging than some of his modern-day colleagues. It's important to remember that, beginning with Freud, many of those interested in the revela-tory possibilities of dreams have concerned themselves to a greater or lesser extent with people who were being treated for psychological or emotional difficulties. Cynics have pointed out that some of Freud's more striking ideas – such as women envying men their penises or wanting sex with their father – may have arisen out of the neuroses of his patients. Some have gone further and suggested that his idea that even very young children have strong sex drives arose because he misinterpreted what he was being told. The fact that Freud always put his patients' stories of sexual encounters with adults during their childhood down to wish-fulfilment, might be because he simply ignored the possi-bility that such sexual abuse of children was rife in Viennese society.

Despite all that, we should not be tempted to underestimate

the importance of Freud's insights. By the nineteenth century, when he began to study dreams in order to understand the psyche, his medical colleagues considered such investigations to be verging on the occult. 'Respectable' doctors at first dismissed his theories completely, and pooh-poohed the whole idea that psychology could offer any benefit or insight to anyone.

Sex and dreams

When it came to considering the role of dreams, Freud was impressed with the work of Artemidorus, but differed from him in believing that it was the dreamer's interpretation that mattered, not the analyst's. Freud's study of his own dreams and those of his patients led him to conclude that they were 'the guardians of sleep'. By this he meant that a person's sleep would otherwise be disturbed by unacceptable thoughts that came to the surface during sleep – mostly consisting of unconscious or repressed sexual desires. Dreaming disguised these unacceptable urges by censoring them and allowing the dreamer to experience their fulfilment in a safer form.

So, according to Freud: 'the content of a dream is a representation of an unfulfilled wish . . . and its obscurity is due to alterations in repressed material made by censorship.'

What this meant was that all dreams needed to be considered on two different levels, and in practice, as two different dreams. The first was what he called the manifest dream – what the sleeper remembered on waking; the second and important one was the so-called latent or true dream which was buried under a protective disguise. The task then facing the dreamer – and his analyst – was to strip away the mask to reveal what the dream was really about. The answer was almost invariably sex!

And if you need more proof of this, you need look no further than Freud's *Introductory Lectures on Psychoanalysis*:

Birth is almost invariably represented by some reference to water: either we are falling into water or clambering out of it, saving someone from it or being saved by them . . . For dying we have setting out on a journey or travelling by train . . . it cannot fail to strike us that objects and matters belonging to another range of ideas are represented by a remarkably rich symbolism. I am speaking of what pertains to the sexual life – the genitals, sexual processes and intercourse. An over- whelming majority of symbols in dreams are sex symbols.

Freud didn't spare himself when it came to dream analysis – in fact it was his painstaking insight into what has become known as his 'Irma dream' that confirmed his opinion of the signifi- cance of dreams. Irma was a patient he had been treating for some time for what Freud considered to be neurotic symptoms, although she complained of stomach pains, and even though she had improved, she had not recovered fully. This fact was commented on to Freud by a colleague, Dr Otto, whose remarks were taken amiss by the great man. He felt they questioned his medical judgement, and wrote out a case history for another medical colleague, Dr M, whom he hoped would back his judge- ment. That night, Freud had a complicated dream featuring his patient and his two medical colleagues, in which she appeared to have signs of physical illness. The other two doctors made suggestions on treating Irma – one of which involved an in- jection – which Freud thought were incorrect.

Rather than accept that his dream was simply a reflection of his worries about Irma and her treatment, Freud looked for an explanation that satisfied his theory that dreams always repre- sented wish-fulfilment. Freud's insistence in his dream that his patient had brought her symptoms on herself, and also that they might have an organic cause, satisfied his wish to believe that the patient's illness was her own problem and not his responsi- bility. He also made connections between Irma's dream symp- toms and underlying sexual difficulties, which fitted in with his idea that this kind of thing was always at the bottom of any neurosis. His criticism of the ideas of the other two doctors reflected his wish to have his judgement vindicated, regardless of the effect this might have on patient or colleagues.

The technique used by Freud and his followers to uncover hidden meanings was called free association, and involved the dreamer coming out with any words that came to mind in connection with his dream. Eventually, this would lead to the real subject of the dream. Suppose, for example, you have dreamed of a cow chewing the cud: one possible trail your thoughts might follow in free association could be: cow – milk – breast – sex, which was usually the end point of many such attempts at explaining a dream, of course!

Although Freud was a trained neurologist, much of the knowledge on which he based his dream theory has now been superseded, and modern Freudian analysts would not accept the idea that all dreams are a disguised fulfilment of erotic desires.

The importance of Jung

The other important founder of modern dream analysis was Freud's younger contemporary and early protégé Carl Jung. His approach to understanding dreams came to differ in important respects from that of Freud as he began developing his own theories. Unlike Freud, who believed that certain symbols in dreams had the same meaning for everyone, Jung felt they must be interpreted anew for each individual. To him, a symbol seen in a dream could have two distinct meanings. One, which would be the same for everyone, was the meaning it had in the collective unconscious – a kind of shared memory bank of thoughts and feelings common to all humans. The second meaning was the personal one which it had for each individual.

He didn't agree with Freud that dreams were deliberately disguised to conceal the unpleasant truth about the dreamer's desires, but thought that the meaning could be uncovered if you looked hard enough. He never thought it would be easy, however: 'If we meditate upon a dream sufficiently long and thoroughly,' he wrote, 'if we carry it around with us and turn it over and over, something almost always comes of it.' He used a technique similar to that of Freud to unravel the confusion by exploring the experiences which might have stimulated a particular dream, but called it amplification rather than free association.

Like his mentor, Jung used a dream of his own to formulate his theory of what dreams in general represent. In his case, the image was of a house, beautifully furnished and comfortable on the top floor, but becoming increasingly less so the further he descended. Ultimately, he reached a primitive cave under the house, where he found old skulls and other vestiges of ancient occupants. For Jung this was a perfect illustration of the structure of the human mind – the top floor representing conscious reality, and the lower levels ever deeper layers of the unconscious mind, reaching right down to the collective unconscious which had its roots in man's earliest history.

Another major difference with Freud was that Jung didn't believe that all dreams were about sex and that all symbolic images must be interpreted in this light. It is said that he once posed the still unresolved question: if things like a tower, a knife or a sword were phallic symbols according to Freudian dream theory, what could a dream of a penis itself actually mean? Jung believed that, while there are many common dream motifs, such as flying or falling, they need to be understood in the light of the dreamer's own experience. This approach is the basis for much dream analysis today.

It's true to say that the work of these two great analysts elevated dreams to the position of something worth serious consideration. What's more, from that point on, thinkers and commentators from several different fields of study have developed their own dream theories. Philosophers, scientists, psychologists and anthropologists have all put in their pennyworth, and you can please yourself what you choose to agree with. As is the way with scientists, about the only thing most pychologists agree on is that dreams are interesting and revealing, although there are some, as we've seen in chapter 2, who don't even accept that much!

The dream controversy

Like Jung, many dream analysts have based their ideas on those of Freud, although in some cases this is only true inasmuch as they are disagreeing with his original theory. Much of the discussion has centred on two main areas. The first is whether there is really a distinction between what the dream appears to be about and its hidden meaning. This refers to what Freud called the 'manifest dream' and the 'latent dream'. The second controversy arises directly from the first, and is about how you think of images in dreams: can we really say that certain symbols have distinct, recognisable meanings for everyone, and if so, what are they?

If you believe, like Freud, that certain symbols have a single meaning for everyone, then presumably it would be a simple matter of looking up the dream in a dream dictionary for everything to become immediately clear. Unfortunately and perhaps inevitably, it's not that simple, as we shall see in chapter 8. Nevertheless, the work of Freud and Jung provoked fascinating controversies which are still being argued out today.

Adler, for example, did not accept the basic Freudian idea that all dreams were disguised wish-fulfilment motivated by a desire to satisfy infantile and/or socially unacceptable desires – having sex with a close friend's partner, for instance. For Adler, dreams were, in part at least, an attempt to solve problems, and looked forward to future development of the person's psyche rather than back to the supposed joys of infancy. He believed that the emotions experienced in a dream could be carried over into waking life, where they could be used to deal with problems the dreamer's rational self had been avoiding.

Several modern analysts have concentrated on making the meaning of dreams more accessible. Conventional Freudian analysis involves weeks – if not years – of regular sessions exploring the psyche with the help of a therapist. The approach of people like Calvin Hall, writing in the 60s, aimed to make what Freud called 'dreamwork' less mysterious and time-consuming, and so more freely available. In particular, this meant looking at the dream experience of healthy as well as sick people in a normal environment rather than a hospital or clinic. He thought that we could extract the meaning from the pictures in our dreams in the same way as we do from the work of artists.

Like Jung, Hall believed that it was much more useful to analyse a series of dreams rather than simply working on each one separately. Using what he called a 'spotlight' approach, he would focus on a basic conflict highlighted in one dream, then see whether and how the same problem expressed itself in other dreams. In his view, symbols actually expressed some thought or emotion in a direct way, and were not messages in disguise. Using this approach, the dreamer could be helped to identify the particular conflict and work through it to a satisfactory resolution.

On the other hand, Fritz Perls, founder of the school of psychotherapy known as Gestalt, thought that the best way to get at the meaning of a dream was to get the person to retell it, acting out different roles and events when possible. In this way, the analyst could use the person's choice of words, body language and tone of voice as additional guides to true understanding. Like Hall, he believed that dreaming could help put us in touch with our inner selves, and so he saw images and symbols as aspects of an individual dreamer's personality, to be interpreted accordingly.

A more complicated view of symbols was advocated by another American psychologist, Thomas French. For him, they could be both universal, with the same meaning for everyone, and functional at the same time. In other words, the normal, everyday purpose of the object in real life could have a bearing on its role in the dream. With these interpretations to guide him, the therapist would then try to set the dream in the context of the person's past life and experience. Like Freud, he would use the technique of free association, making use of intuition to relate the dream's message to the dreamer's current emotional state.

Although there have been a lot of voices raised in opposition to Freud's approach to dreams, he has his supporters too. The psychoanalytic approach to dreaming is still popular today, especially in the USA, even though not in its original, pure form. In the 1950s, Erik Erikson devised a systematic approach to Freudian-type analysis, giving more weight to the manifest dream – or what the dreamer actually said his dream was about. He pointed out that this was more than just a disguise for much more unpleasant desires, since it was a real reflection of the person's current concerns. Psychologist David Foulkes has developed Freud's concept of the manifest and latent dream into a method of using free association to uncover the hidden meaning buried in a patient's account of his dream.

Charles Rycroft, a British psychoanalyst, takes a broader view, and is not prepared to accept that dreams are all about fulfilling wishes which are too awful to contemplate in real life. He doesn't dismiss the aspect of wish-fulfilment entirely, but prefers to concentrate on the creative and positive elements of dreams. Other modern psychoanalysts would agree in seeing a dream as the transformation of hidden hopes, wishes or experiences, rather than as a disguised or censored version of the true meaning. This change of emphasis allows them to see dreams as a way of expressing a particular idea or feeling, or even as a creative insight, and not simply as a way of concealing 'something nasty in the woodshed'.

American psychoanalyst Dr Robert Langs believes that while the surface of our dreams – the jumble we remember – is inevitably puzzling, it conceals a deeper layer of meaning which relates to events in our real lives. According to Dr Langs, while the conscious mind is getting on with its task of coping with everyday existence, the unconscious mind is trying to bring repressed worries to the surface so they can be dealt with. Often, therefore, there is something unpleasant like guilt or sexual dissatisfaction trying to gain expression through dreams. Although universal Freudian-type symbols may have some part to play here, according to Dr Langs we can only hope to uncover the true meaning of our dreams by looking at our real lives.

To explain his theory in more detail, he gives as an example the story of a young woman who had a horrifying dream of a man trying to harm her. Shortly afterwards, her husband told her he was having an affair and wanted to leave her. Dr Langs explains the dream as a sign that the woman had unconsciously picked up – and ignored – indications that something was wrong in her relationship with her husband. The dream showed that her unconscious mind was trying to bring the problem to the surface so it could be tackled and resolved.

Modern dream research has made numerous attempts at finding an explanation of dreaming which makes sense both of scientific findings and psychological approaches. The general idea behind such theories is that dreams are in some way allowing us the opportunity to unite early memories and ways of behaving, either learnt in childhood or possibly even inborn, with more recent experiences. The French psychologist Jouvet has suggested that dreams are the mechanism by which we reconcile instinctive behaviour with what we have learned in everyday life.

The modern interpreters

Interesting though these theories may be, it's all too easy to get bogged down in the subtleties of their arguments. Thinking in terms of unresolved conflicts or repressed desires being covertly acted out is enough to turn you into a neurotic in itself. Many modern dream interpreters take a less intense and somewhat more upbeat appraoch to a subject which fascinates us all. We don't have to believe that we are suffering from some hidden or deep-seated problem which our dreams may explain. Rather, we simply want to know what lies behind the chaos and strange goings-on which occupy us at night. We probably ask ourselves such questions like 'What on earth made me dream of her?' or 'Why was I trying to get to Manchester on a cross-Channel ferry?' The answers are bound to be intriguing, even if they don't shed any blinding light on our childhood experiences or hidden ambitions.

Much modern dream interpretation deals with the subject more on this level but it can still be quite revealing about what's really on our minds.

Dream workshops are, as we might expect, very popular in parts of the USA, and becoming more so as the study of dreams fits naturally into the whole 'New Age' approach to understanding ourselves and our relation to others. One well-known practitioner explains that the 1990s were under the influence of the planet Pluto, which rules the unconscious, bringing forward everything that we have buried and don't want to face up to. She and other people who work in a similar way believe that learning to understand our dreams can open up a whole new world, connecting us to our past, present and future. They can thus help us to understand ourselves, solve problems and even enhance our creativity.

Apart from drawing on their own experience and the theories of their chosen experts, 'New Agers' also bring into play the experiences of other cultures. This may range from stories of 'the Dreamtime', which is part of the spiritual beliefs of the Australian Aboriginals, to the dreamwork of the Senoi, a primitive tribe living in Malaysia in the early part of this century. They are renowned amongst dream analysts for their sound psychological health, which was said, before their culture was destroyed, to stem in large part from their reliance on dream experience to guide their daily life and relations with one another.

So, clearly interpreting your dreams is as much about what you know and experience as what you believe about the meaning and role of dreams in your life. And having an open mind which takes into account a wide range of possible explanations is clearly the first step towards getting the most out of your own dreams and what they could mean for you.

4

the history of
dreams

Whatever the experts conclude that dreams truly are, one thing is for sure – they have always fascinated us. At different times in our history, they have been seen as warnings or messages from the gods, supernatural experiences involving visions of the future and indications of the sleeper's problems – both physical and mental. And we think it's perfectly normal today to swap stories over breakfast or in conversation with friends, and happily theorise as to what they might mean. Even in the sophisticated twentieth century, we accept them without question in plays, novels and TV programmes – although credibility was recently stretched to its limits by the writers of *Dallas*.

When Pam Ewing woke to the sound of Bobby singing in the shower, and eventually she (and we) realised that Bobby wasn't dead after all, many dedicated viewers felt just slightly conned. After all, we'd all been sharing the many and various dramas with the characters only to find that our interest and concern had been wasted: it had all happened in Pam's dream and wasn't 'real' at all! Could it be, we asked ourselves, that the dream device was a plot to arrest falling ratings rather than a convincing development of the storyline – a plot within a plot, as it were?

But this is not the only example of celluloid fantasies crossing over into the elusive world of our dreams. Some years ago, psychologist and dream researcher Christopher Evans asked readers of a variety of magazines which films they felt came closest to their own experiences of dreams. He found the answers fascinating, with some predictable candidates and others – such as *Lassie Come Home* – rather more surprising. Along with those which had deliberately imitated the strange time scale and illogical nature of dreams, like the cult French film *L'année dernière à Marienbad*, were others like the Beatles' *Yellow submarine* and Jonathan Miller's TV version of *Alice in Wonderland*. As Evans pointed out, this sheds an interesting light on what some people apparently get up to in their dreams! There were some differences between men and women too, the male top choice being Kubrick's *2001*, while more women recognised a dreamlike quality in *Dr Zhivago*.

People have always understood and used dreams in different ways according to the beliefs of the society they lived in. From that point of view, it perhaps isn't surprising that Dr Chris Hanning, a sleep researcher at the University of Leicester, describes them as 'an internal video system to keep us amused at night'. In earlier ages, dreams would feature naturally in stories, where they were often used to explain events and individuals' motives in behaving as they did.

Dream stories from the past

About the earliest known example is in a book called *The Epic of Gilgamesh*, the story of which was probably told aloud long before it was written down. Some time in the third millennium BC in the area that is now in southern Iraq, lived the great King Gilgamesh of Uruk, who was 'strong as a savage bull'. To help contain his energies, a goddess created another man to be Gilgamesh's equal and friend. Before the two met, Gilgamesh dreamed strange dreams, one of a meteor which fell to earth, and another of an axe which drew him to it 'like the love of a woman'. His mother interpreted them for him, saying, 'What you have seen, this star of Heaven . . . this was the strong comrade, the one who brings help to his friend in need. . . . That axe . . . is the comrade whom I shall give you, and he will come in his strength like one of the host of heaven.'

The prediction comes true, and King Gilgamesh and his friend Enkidu go on to have heroic and tragic adventures, in which dreams and their interpretation play a crucial part. This five-thousand-year-old story is the first recorded instance of dreams being seen as influencing people's lives, sometimes by predicting the future and by conveying messages from the gods to chosen mortals.

The Ancient Egyptians and Greeks, too, accepted the idea that the gods would reveal themselves to ordinary people in dreams, often with news of what was to happen to them. In Ancient Greece, epic stories of war, adventure at sea, love and revenge were probably told aloud long before they were written down. The stories of the Greeks' war with Troy and its after-math have survived in the *Odyssey* and the *Iliad*, probably written by the poet Homer in the tenth century BC. Dreams and their consequences play a big part in the action, although there was often little need of interpretation because the messages were clear and not disguised in symbols. Nevertheless, Homer distinguished between 'true' dreams, which the dreamer should act on, and 'evil' dreams which could deceive the dreamer into doing the wrong thing. In the *Odyssey*, he explained that:

> *Two gates for ghostly dreams there are: one gateway*
> *of honest horn, and one of ivory.*
> *Issuing by the ivory gates are dreams*

of glimmering illusion, fantasies,
but those that come through solid polished horn
may be borne out, if mortals only know them.

A good dream could obviously resolve all kinds of problems – and came in handy to move his story along too!

For example, the *Odyssey* tells how the goddess Athene took pity on Odysseus' wife Penelope, who was worried about a murder plot against her son Telemachus and appeared to her in a dream. In true, dreamlike fashion, however, the goddess took on the appearance of Penelope's sister, who passed on the message that Telemachus would survive. Sensibly taking the opportunity to fill in another gap in her knowledge, Penelope asked her dream sister whether her husband – Telemachus' father Odysseus – was also still alive, as she had heard nothing from him since he had gone off to the Trojan War. Typically, the messenger claimed to know nothing about this, and disappeared instantly. Dreams, it seems, were just as frustrating then as they are now!

Even then, some writers thought there was more to dreams than messages from the gods or a useful way to advance the plot. Plato's view sounds almost as though it could have been written by Sigmund Freud some two thousand years later. In his *Republic* he said: ' . . . in fact, there exists in every one of us, even in some reputed most respectable, a terrible, fierce and lawless brood of desires, which it seems are revealed in our sleep.'

One of the earliest guides to dream interpretation was written by a Greek in the second century BC. Artemidorus took a remarkably sophisticated view of what dreams were all about, realising that they could and should be interpreted in different ways according to individual circumstances. He also took into account the feelings of the dreamer, their occupation and the circumstances in which they had the dream. His interpretations would often be based on a series of dreams, and he regarded the imagery as symbols with hidden meanings which had to be teased out.

When a dream was a warning

Like the Homeric Greeks, the Ancient Egyptians would ask questions of their gods, who might choose to appear with the answers in a dream. However, they were not above interfering in human lives without invitation – and were believed to send warnings and instructions through men's dreams when they felt it necessary. They might demand that the dreamer repent some evil action or put right its consequences, but they sometimes also brought warnings of troubles to come.

Like us, the Egyptians looked for help in understanding their dreams, and expert interpreters were attached to many of the temples dedicated to Serapis, the Egyptian god of dreams. Excavations in Memphis found an inscription over a door to a room used by one of these analysts which reads:

I interpret dreams, having the gods' mandate to do so. Good luck to you if you enter here.

The idea that a dream could be a warning from God of danger ahead was carried through into the Christian era. According to the Gospel of St Matthew, the three Wise Men, following their star to find the baby Jesus, had consulted Herod, King of Judaea, about where they would find Jesus. Herod asked them to continue their search, then let him know when they succeeded, 'that I may come and worship him also'. However, St Matthew comments in passing that the three Wise Men ignored this request: 'being warned of God in a dream that they should not return to Herod, they departed into their own country another way.'

The Evangelist apparently felt no need to explain such behaviour, taking it for granted that sensible people would act upon this form of communication.

Later, however, insight into the meaning of dreams was put to more sinister use by the infamous Inquisition – the Church's 'thought police'. The judges took it upon themselves to put particular interpretations on the dreams of those accused of witch-craft, and then used this to condemn them to be burned at the stake! It goes without saying that the victims' ideas of what their dreams meant counted for nothing in these circumstances.

While it obviously suited the inquisitors to take this line, their suspicious approach reflected the fact that many people distrusted the message of dreams. They suspected that the devil had a hand in them as often as not, and used them to fool sleepers into dastardly acts.

Dreams as power

Dreams have always been used for their own purposes by those in power, whether from genuine belief or as a means to an end. Even in relatively modern times, Adolf Hitler would sometimes base decisions on interpretations of his dreams provided by his personal dream analysts. As with absolute rulers in earlier centuries, however, it would be a brave or even foolhardy analyst who offered an interpretation which contradicted the Fuhrer's known beliefs and policies. This was likely to lead to sudden termination of employment – or worse!

While those in positions of power might choose to give their dreams great weight and authority, the chances were that, in reality, they and their subjects had a rather more ambivalent atti-tude to the significance of their sleep experiences. The best analogy is with the way we regard astrology today. While at one end of the spectrum there are those who treat the subject with enormous seriousness, and at the other there are those who regard the whole thing as complete nonsense, the majority of us fall somewhere in between these two extremes. We know our star signs and read our horoscopes, and are sometimes struck by their apparent accuracy. Nevertheless, if someone were to ask us next day what the stars foretold for us this week or month, we probably wouldn't remember very much of what we'd read.

You'll often hear people say that they don't get on with

someone else 'because she's a Saggitarius', for example, or that you can't believe everything so-and-so says 'because she's a Gemini and they're very two-faced'. Astrology is a part of our culture, and most people know a bit about it but we rarely base real decisions or form relationships purely on the basis of what the stars tell us.

It was probably much the same with dreams in earlier centuries. People would understand that dreams were supposed to have significance, and might well discuss the omens and portents they'd seen, but would nevertheless go about their business largely disregarding this knowledge.

As with astrology today, however, there were no doubt important exceptions to this generalisation. Many people were shocked to discover a few years ago that the American First Lady, Nancy Reagan, regularly consulted an astrologer to advise her about plans and decisions faced by the most powerful ruler in the Western world – and apparently took the advice seriously.

Some people were reminded of the scene in Shakespeare's *Julius Caesar* in which Caesar's wife tries to dissuade him from going to the Roman Senate because she's had a dream foretelling that something terrible will happen if he does. Interestingly, Shakespeare, writing from the perspective of a sixteenth-century Englishman, has Caesar dismiss Calpurnia's concerns and stick to his original plan – which ends disastrously, as she has foretold, with his assassination. We can speculate whether this means that Shakespeare was intending to reinforce the belief in predictive dreams and the dangers of ignoring them, or whether he simply thought that the Ancient Romans were a superstitious lot and bloodthirsty with it!

The literature of our dreams

As this example illustrates, we are definitely on shaky ground in trying to use literature as a way of assessing how our forbears thought about dreams and their importance. One of the best-known instances of dreams playing a role in the creative process is now considered more than a little suspect. The poet Samuel Taylor Coleridge claimed that his famous poem *Kubla Khan* had come to him word-for-word while he was dreaming under the influence of a bedtime dose of opium. Unfortunately, he had only managed to write down the first fifty or so lines when he was interrupted by a vistor he referred to as 'a person from Porlock' wanting to see him on business. By the time he had been dealt with, claimed Coleridge, the rest of the poem had vanished from his mind in the way that dreams do, so he was never able to finish it.

It was an astonishing story, but sadly it was almost certainly untrue – or at best a gross exaggeration. The poem – and the explanation of its origins – were not revealed publicly until twenty years after the supposed dream in 1797, and many critics today believe that the poet had actually been working on it in the intervening time.

Lord Tennyson, too, is said to have dreamed great chunks of poetry, but he was either more forgetful or more honest than Coleridge in that he never claimed to have based any of his subsequent works on them. He managed to produce only four lines of a dream poem, experienced at the age of 10, but the rest he simply forgot – just like the rest of us!

Many nineteenth-century writers used dreams as a source of inspiration, although without claiming that the whole form of their work had been revealed at one go. It may say something about the nature of dream inspiration that much of the litera-ture apparently derived from it falls into the general category of horror stories. Robert Louis Stevenson is said to have dreamed the plot of *The Strange Case of Dr Jekyll and Mister Hyde*, while Mary Shelley based her classic *Frankenstein* on such an experi-ence. Writing afterwards of her dream inspiration, she conjured up a horrible picture:

> *I saw the pale student of unhallowed arts kneeling beside the thing he had put together. I saw the hideous phantasm of a*

43

man stretched out, and then, on the working of some powerful engine, show signs of life, and stir with an uneasy, half vital motion.

She sensibly concluded that a scene which had thoroughly frightened her would certainly do the same for her readers, and we are still being frightened by variations of her story today.

These writers, like their counterparts throughout history, were undoubtedly influenced by the ideas current in their time. Many philosophers have looked at dreams in the course of their thinking, especially those whose preoccupation was with what is real and what we can know about ourselves and the external world.

In particular, thinkers like the eighteenth-century philosopher Descartes were concerned as to how we could distinguish between reality and the products of our minds. This idea was anticipated thousands of years before by the Chinese philosopher Chwang-Tse who had a vivid dream that he was a butterfly. He recorded his experience and the question it provoked:

Once upon a time, I, Chwang-Tse, dreamed I was a butterfly, fluttering hither and thither, to all intents and purposes a butterfly. I was aware only of following my fancy as a butterfly and unconscious of my human individuality. Suddenly, I awoke, and there I lay, myself again. Now I do not know whether I was then a man dreaming I was a butterfly or whether I am now a butterfly dreaming I am a man.

The same problem preoccupied Lewis Carroll, as is evident from the scene in *Alice in Wonderland*, when she and Tweedledee are discussing the dreaming Tweedledum. Tweedledee announces that Tweedledum is dreaming of Alice, then asks her:

'And if he left off dreaming about you, where do you suppose you'd be?'
'Where I am now, of course,' said Alice.

'Not you!' Tweedledee retorted contemptuously. 'You'd be nowhere. Why, you're only a sort of thing in his dream!'

Perhaps it shouldn't come as a surprise that this confusion, once suffered by a Chinese philosopher far distant in time and culture from us, is still something we can identify with today. We have all had dreams that were so memorable that they seemed to haunt us and invade our everyday lives for a long time afterwards. It's almost as if the events are something we remember happening rather than a figment of our imagination.

'All this we see or seem is but a dream within a dream,' wrote the American novelist Edgar Allan Poe. And the truth of the matter is that, with all the scientific advances in recent years, we still haven't managed to unveil the mystery that is our dream-life.

6

the secret world
of your dreams

In an average lifetime, we can expect to dream for about 50,000 hours – which is an awful lot of dreaming! And considering that around a quarter of our sleep is REM sleep – that notches up about ninety minutes a night – it's no wonder that dreaming has occupied the time and minds of so many experts.

Whether the actual process of dreaming performs a specific function is, as we've seen, a hotly debated area among scientists. Interestingly, while Freud believed, 'The interpretation of dreams is the royal road to a knowledge of the unconscious activities of the mind,' Dr Charles Fisher, in *The Senses of Animals and Men*, wrote 'Dreaming permits each and every one of us to be quietly and safely insane every night of our lives.'

Whichever way you look at it, dreaming plays a part in all of our lives; the only difference is what we dream and how much we actually remember when we wake up. As we've already seen there are various explanations as to why some of us seem to have better powers of recall than others: some experts say it's down to whether you've been woken suddenly during a period of REM sleep, others suggest that we're not 'programmed' to remember, while one theory is that our night-time stories are often too mundane for us to bother remembering anything about them! So, when we're going through a relatively boring phase in our lives, we may remember more, whilst when our days are more eventful, the chances are that we remember less.

Theories abound as to what the dreams actually mean: maybe they're the result of our repressing something in our lives; they could be a symptom of stress; a way of fulfilling our daytime dreams and fantasies; an attempt at solving problems; or even our mind's attempt at sorting out the debris (the minor details and seemingly insignificant events) of the day.

Some experts believe that even nightmares have a role to play in our lives, as the negative images can be used in a positive way to help the dreamer confront – and ultimately conquer – his fears. In truth, why we've dreamt in the first place, and what it means, is likely to involve an amalgam of factors – all depending on the dream and on our present state of mind. So, in many ways dreaming is simply the language of our mind.

Whatever theory you consider most likely, there's no denying that dreams do have a role to play. Physically and physiologically it's been shown that we can suffer if we have to go withour our REM sleep. Our bodies need it and if deprived of our nightly viewing our body quickly makes up for it by jamming in extra REM sessions at the first available opportunity. So although we may talk about 'catching up' on our sleep after a few late nights, what's more likely is that we're catching up on our REM sleep.

In one study, a group of students was monitored over a period of one night. Just before they were about to go to sleep, researchers presented them with a problem. The students were then left to fall sleep. However, some were allowed to sleep uninterrupted, whilst the others were woken during their REM, or dreaming, sleep. Interestingly, the researchers discovered that the group whose dreams were uninterrupted had a much better idea of how to solve the bedtime problem than the other group. However, whether this fact was down to the simple explanation that group one wasn't suffering from lack of sleep generally, compared to group two, wasn't actually tested.

For therapists past and present, dreams have had a significant part to play in understanding the complexities of their patients' minds. Psychologists have recognised for years that the more disturbed someone is, the greater chance there is of them experiencing vivid and distressing dreams. And it isn't just adults: this holds true for children too.

However, you don't have to be suffering prolonged periods of mental anguish to benefit from understanding your dreams. Our nocturnal meanderings may contribute to our overall self-development, as well as helping us to gain an insight into previously unexplored territories. They may help you to reassess a situation or even force you to confront a particular problem that you have been trying to ignore. And, in the late twentieth century, with a new emphasis on self-awareness and personal development, understanding our dreams may well have a far greater part to play than was previously thought.

Whatever theory you feel is the most likely, it's hard to believe that there's no purpose at all to so much subconscious activity. And with philosophers from Plato to Aristotle, and poets and writers like Samuel Taylor Coleridge and Robert Louis Stevenson all claiming that dreams have a significant part to play, it shows that dreaming can sometimes be as useful as it is enjoyable. What's more, with around one and a half hours spent doing it every night, it would seem a shame not to at least try to make the most of it!

Common ground

Although dreaming is an individual business – a little like a memo written to you, from you, in a type of shorthand that is only really fully understood by you – on the whole, the dreams themselves do cover a surprising amount of common ground. One American study showed that at least one other familiar person appears in almost all our dreams and in around a third of dreams these people, or the dreamer himself, are active in some way – whether speaking, listening or looking at something. In another third of the group, the people being dreamt about are moving, whilst physical activity generally was discovered not to seem like hard work.

Maybe not too surprisingly, the menial tasks of our daily lives were rarely depicted (well, given the choice would you want to dream of doing the ironing?), although what we dream is more likely to be negative than positive. One third of the dreamers noted feelings of fear and anxiety and it seems that unhappiness, defeat and failure seem to occur more often than happiness and contentment.

Happier emotions are less common in dreams and, sadly, hostile and aggressive events are considerably more common than friendly ones. Oddly, the same American study also discovered that even when dreams contain events and occasions that in our non-dream world would cause excitement and exhilaration, the feelings are likely to be considerably subdued, almost reducing the dreamer to the role of voyeur – even when he is the primary subject of the dream.

However, it's worth remembering that when we wake up and start to go through the memories of the night, what we're actually remembering is a snapshot of the dream, not the whole dream. And the images that we remember are almost subconsciously put into some sort of order. We 'edit' them into sense but the way we define that sense is very personal and determined by the sort of person we are and the situation we are in. So, we find the meaning that suits us, even though the initial dream may well contain a jumbled catalogue of events, often totally unrelated, and sometimes even ludicrous.

In fact one of the essential differences between our waking

and dreaming worlds is that in the former there is a logic to events and associations, whereas – as all dreamers everywhere can testify – this is not necessarily the case when we aren't awake! In your waking world if you invite someone for tea, when the doorbell rings you know that it's the friend or relative you've been expecting. But in the dream world you may suddenly find yourself taking tea with the Queen – for no apparent reason – or going to the cinema with Harrison Ford!

In the same way, when we think back on our waking day, we only remember the 'edited' highlights, often subconsciously filtering out the minutiae: uneventful activities – like how many streets you needed to walk down to get to the station, how many different types of pasta were on offer in the supermarket, or how many people you passed on the escalator as you walked up the steps. But it's worth bearing in mind that while a dream may mean very little to someone who doesn't know you, the images it has conjured up can evoke a lifetime of memories for you, personally.

It follows then that every dream is interpreted differently for each individual because our dreams reflect our relationship to any given experience that we might have. So we impose a plot on a sequence of events, and the more creative we are, the more likely we are to turn it into a story. And, it also follows that the more sensitive we are to the material, the more likely it will determine exactly how much we will actually get out of our dreams.

Think of it this way: imagine you're watching television, or maybe a play. The material can be broken down into a sequence of images, each one representing a part of the story. Now, you can be a passive viewer or an active one. A passive viewer is the person who is slumped in front of the players, mildly acknowledging the action but, like some innocent bystander, emotionally uninvolved. Alternatively, you may concentrate hard on the images passing before you, mentally piecing events and scenes together, making connections between the plot and sub-plot and, along with the characters, decoding the symbols as events unravel. So, in a sense, the more you put into understanding your dreams, the more likely you are to gain something positive out of it.

Clearly our dreams are our own creation – a product of our thoughts, our culture, our experience. It's also been shown, on successive occasions, that the dream is almost always formed by an event that has happened in the last twenty-four hours. The event – however seemingly insignificant – acts as a trigger, even if only by association. You may dream of an old school-friend who you haven't seen for years. While you haven't had direct contact with this friend, you may have spoken to another friend – unconnected with the old friend – who mentioned that she was thinking of organising a reunion for her old class. Subconsciously you had stored that information, and the conversation had acted as a trigger for your own dream, containing your own 'cast list'.

Content and context

Most dreams can be divided into content and context: whilst the content may well be determined by a recent phone-call, film or an unscheduled encounter, the context in which the dream takes place may well be an indicator of your personal state of mind. If we return for a minute to the play, or programme, analogy: the scene in which the play takes place is less import-ant than how the play's characters react emotionally to what's going on. And if we work on the basis that our dreams function on two levels, then the initial level may deal with basic thoughts and observations, while the second, deeper level deals with our worries and obsessions.

Consequently, it's important not to generalise or make sweeping assumptions about the meaning of a dream, particu-larly if it appears as a complex web of events and people, with tenuous associations, all set in surreal circumstances. Each individual has their own set of associations that adds an extra dimension to the dream and therefore the meaning lies within that person. In fact, one commentator likened dreams to an iceberg which only reveals a small part of the whole: it's below the water level where the real meaning lies.

Of course dream interpretation would be so much easier if it was all simply down to associating a certain image with a particular event. For example, if you were to dream of eating poison ivy, wouldn't it be simple if we could conclude that this means that you can expect a sudden illness? Unfortunately, it just doesn't work like that! In many cases the dreamer is as important, if not more, than the content of the dream itself and it's the dreamer alone who holds the key to understanding the secrets of REM sleep.

Let's take another example. If you dreamt about an aeroplane, and then looked this image up and, surprise, surprise, it told you that you were going on a journey, in no time at all you'd have your definitive interpretation – particularly if it was during holiday time. End of story. But hold on – is it really? Once you think beyond the initial image, and give some thought to the significance that going away, or even flying itself, has to you, you'll see that the picture immediately starts to change. So, just suppose you know someone who was hurt in an accident whilst on holiday, or your family lives on the other side of the world, or you have an innate fear of flying? Obviously the image of an aeroplane begins to take on a completely different meaning from the initial one, once the dreamer's own emotional history and individual complexities are put into the mix.

Without doubt, dreaming is a highly complex business. Generally speaking, we dream about what we experience, thoughts as well as actions, although neither need be firsthand. You may never have visited the Eiffel Tower, but it's almost certain that you've seen enough representations of it, either through films or toy-sized models, to feel that you have seen it. The same is true of prison. While the majority of us haven't been detained at Her Majesty's pleasure, most of us are still familiar with the endless corridors, the almost deafening silence as the clang of hefty steel doors signals lock-up time, and the swilling of buckets that can only mean slopping out. The images are often so strong that firsthand experience seems almost irrelevant.

Interference

Not too surprisingly dreams change as we do: they continually reflect the lives we lead and the experiences that we're exposed to, whether dramatic or mundane. However, some of the material that our sleep-time stories cover can be dictated by external circumstances, in the same way that the sound of a radio can become distorted by electrical interference. So it's important always to acknowledge the possibility of this kind of interference distorting your dreams.

After all, most of us have at least one sub-plot going on in our lives: even the subjects who take part in laboratory dream monitoring may set out calmly for a night's sleep, only to arrive in a state of extreme agitation due to a steaming row with their partner. And even though it may have been about something relatively insignificant that is easily resolved and quickly forgotten, it could well be that the incident, while unresolved, will result in streams of unconscious thought, which in turn may seep into the world of their dreams.

Clearly events that we're conscious of can play a part in our REM sleep, but 'interference' doesn't stop there. Something as innocuous as a telephone ringing when you're dreaming can easily be incorporated into the story by the dreamer translating it into the clang of a fire alarm, and depending on your imagination, you could find yourself in the middle of a Towering Inferno, with you and Steve McQueen leading the firefighting! Equally, the beeping of a car's horn in the distance can easily become part of a dream, as could the sound of music or a rude awakening triggered by the alarm going off.

But it isn't only sound that can stimulate our dreams. Sensory stimulation – what we feel – can also play a part. The most famous example of this concerns Alfred Maury, a Frenchman who, in the 1860s, wrote of his dream that was set in the French Revolution towards the end of the eighteenth century. The dream actually involved him being tried, prosecuted and eventually being sent to the guillotine. So vivid was the dream that Maury 'felt' the blade of the guillotine as it severed his head from his body – at which point he awoke, not too surprisingly, in utter horror. However, the most fascinating aspect of Maury's dream was that, when he did wake up, he discovered that the head-board of his bed had somehow become loose and fallen off, hitting him on his neck, presumably at the same place that the guillotine had fallen.

The ability to influence dreams has long since been acknowledged and many sleep clinics have attempted to assess just how strong these influences are. One experiment involved spraying water on individuals, either on their body or face, during their REM sleep to see to what extent it would affect their dreaming. Their findings proved that many of the people incorporated the water into their dreaming, mostly in perfectly straightforward ways, such as spilling a glass of cold water on themselves.

Even in non-laboratory conditions people have reported a connection between dreams and physical sensations. One of the most common is a dream where you find yourself in Arctic conditions and then wake up to discover your covers have slipped on to the floor. Other contemporary stories involve dreaming of crossing the Sahara under the burning sun – all due to an electric blanket being left on. That said, however much external elements may play a part in triggering a particular type of dream, it appears that the content of the dream itself is determined by our individual personality. Freud himself was thought to have explored the link between sensations and REM sleep and on one occasion, the night after eating anchovies, which are known for their saltiness, he dreamt of drinking water.

Thirst, hunger, even the need to go to the toilet, can all become the stuff of dreams. One American study involved a group who were deprived of food and liquid for around eight hours before arriving at the laboratory for a night of monitored sleep. The number of dreams about liquids not only increased, but those who dreamt that their thirst was satisfied drank less the next morning than those people whose thirst persisted throughout their dream.

Other less subtle factors can also have some bearing on our dreams and before we can set about trying to understand them, it's important to sort out how much of the meaning can actually be attributed to one isolated factor. Many of us are familiar with the vivid, often distorted, images of dreams that follow an evening where too much eating and, in particular, too much drinking took place. Medication, too, can have an effect, as can a raised temperature or a particularly acute emotional trauma. Eating cheese before bedtime has long been thought of as a dream trigger, although many experts nowadays think that it's more likely to be due to indigestion caused by eating the cheese rather than the cheese itself.

There's also an increased chance that something you've seen in a disturbing TV programme, or film may subtly influence the events that occur in your REM sleep. One study that explored this area involved taking two groups and showing each one a different film, just before bedtime. One film was a particularly brutal and aggressive Western that contained some explicit scenes of violence. By contrast, the other was a lighthearted, romantic comedy. What was interesting was that the researchers discovered that while specific elements of the films had very little influence on the content of the dreams, there seemed to be a noticeable difference in the way the groups dreamed. The dreams that followed the Western were significantly more vivid, imaginative and intense than the dreams that were reported by the group that had seen the comedy.

Another factor to be aware of before hidden meanings are looked for too deeply in a dream is any obvious self-denial that is going on during the waking hours. Ex-smokers are renowned for dreaming either of having a sneaky cigarette or some smoke-related dream – as you'll see in chapter 8. It's very much open to question whether this is due to wish-fulfilment ('I could really do with a cigarette . . .') or repression ('I mustn't give in'), where thoughts of smoking are banished from the mind during the day and so ultimately surface at night when we aren't able to exercise quite as much control over our thoughts and desires.

The road to understanding

Once you've worked out how to distinguish between the dreams that are worth understanding and the ones that are due more to indigestion than inspiration, you then have to set about trying to tap into, as well as document, the material that is the 'stuff' of our dreams.

It may sound obvious, but before you can actually make any sense of your dreams, the first thing you have to do is remember them! And it's a task that may be more difficult than you think. Some experts suggest that before you go to sleep at night you say to yourself several times, 'I will remember my dreams, I will remember my dreams'. Then concentrate hard on the sentence so that it becomes one of the last things you do remember before you begin to fall asleep. And when you wake, train yourself to lie perfectly still for several minutes, contemplating the dream, if necessary making a conscious effort to conjure up the images.

Apparently, while we can all recall at least one dream that was so vivid and powerful that the images and the feelings it left us with seemed to stay with us for days, this is hardly a normal, day-to-day occurrence. Normally, while you may wake during the night and instantly remember your dream, by the time morning comes, you have only a vague idea of what it was about. In fact, it's far more likely that you won't even remember that you actually had a dream at all, however vivid it was at the time.

As we saw in chapter 2, as well as influencing the content of your dreams, any external 'interference' as you're waking will weaken or even destroy your powers of recall. So, if for instance you are woken by a radio alarm, and you find that your powers of consciousness are eased into the waking world either by music, a DJ's ramblings or even reports on the day's news, those memories of the previous night's dreaming are likely to dissolve almost instantly in the stream of sound.

Recording the dream

Consequently it's important that, wherever possible, you take steps to aid your memory recall. Dream analysts recommend that crucial to any attempt at remembering dreams is to keep a notebook, or dream diary, by your bed. Then, whenever you wake up, while the dream is fresh in your mind, you record it. Train yourself to do this as soon as you start to remember – regardless of whether it's first thing in the morning or the middle of the night. In fact, if it's the latter there's probably even more reason to jot it down, because there probably won't be too many people around at that time on to whom you can unload your memories!

And don't fall into the trap of believing that you can scribble down some notes on the night-time's activity once you've woken up properly, had a shower, grabbed a coffee – or whatever you generally do in the morning to help your brain get into gear! In most things, once we've given ourselves time to 'come to' in the morning our brains tend to operate more sharply and we do think more clearly. Where dreams are concerned, however, all the evidence indicates that the more conscious we are in our waking lives, the less conscious we are of our dream world – unless it has been particularly vivid or dramatic. So, do try to remember to record everything you can recall the minute you wake. You'll be surprised to find that after doing this for a week or so you automatically reach for your pen when you wake, regardless of the time.

But what if you're one of those people who almost always seem to find it difficult to remember what you've dreamt? Well don't worry, because, to a certain extent, remembering your dreams is mainly a matter of training yourself to do so. And once you've made up your mind that you do want to remember, you're half-way there. In fact, it's been shown that the more motivated you are to remember, the more chance there is that you'll be successful. Furthermore, one American study discovered that introspective people seem to recall dreaming more easily than people who rarely contemplate their own thoughts and emotions. But this perhaps isn't surprising in view of the fact that those who are introspective are naturally more focused on their inner world.

As well as recording generally what the dream was about you need to be a little analytical. First date each dream, making a note of the time. Then ask yourself the following questions:

- Was there anything significant in the dream?

- Who were the majority of the people? Did you recognise anyone?

- Were there any objects that were memorable?

- Were there any key words or phrases?

- How did you feel during the dream?

- Have you dreamt anything like this before?

- Was colour, season or time of day relevant?

Now, record the dreams but write only on the right side of the notebook. On the left-hand side, either in the evening, or just before you go to bed, jot down some notes to remind yourself about the type of day you've had, paying attention to the particular as well as the general. You need to ask yourself:

- Did anything significant happen today?

- Was there anything that happened that was different?

- Did anything unexpected happen?

- Were there any surprising meetings – maybe with friends or relatives?

- Were they any surprising phone-calls?

- Were you upset by anything, or anyone?

- What sort of a day was it emotionally?

- Is anything worrying or irritating you?

It may sound like a lot of ground to cover but in fact most of the questions could probably be answered in a couple of sentences. It really isn't necessary to write very much, and if you're short of time a couple of key phrases or words will do; just enough to remind you of the sort of day you've had.

The idea behind contrasting your day's events with the stuff of your dreams is to allow you to explore any obvious overlap. It will also mean that you have enough notes to go back over your dreams and discover whether there is a pattern to your dreaming, either in terms of events or themes. On a very basic level you may suddenly realise that there is a direct link between the type of dreams you have and the sort of TV programmes or books you watch or read before you go to bed. And once that's been established, it's fairly simple to work out what you need to do to avoid those sorts of dreams.

Try to keep your notes to no more than a page because this will enable you to compare, directly, with the notes from your dream which you record when you wake up. It's also useful to leave a couple of lines at the bottom of either one, or both, pages so that you can jot down any possible links that might occur to you once you put the two pages together. You may even find that, over the weeks or months, there is a repeated link or theme.

So, an example of how your dream diary may look could be something like this:

What happened today:	**What I dreamt:**
Significant events:	*Significant events:*
_____	_____
_____	_____
_____	_____
People:	*People:*
_____	_____
_____	_____
Significant info:	*Any obvious influences/ connections:*
_____	_____
_____	_____
Progs/Films:	
_____	_____
_____	_____

Stresses: *How I felt:*

_____   _____

_____   _____

Other info: *Other info:*

_____   _____

_____   _____

                    Possible links:

_____

_____

_____

Obviously you should divide the page into sections that suit you – you'll know the key words that are most likely to help you remember either what happened during your waking memories or dreaming ones. What you really want to be able to discover is, are there any obvious links between the day's activities and the events that take place in your dreams?

Making the connection

Once you've got into the habit of recording your dreams, you need to start looking for associations – from dream to dream as well as dream to daytime. Think of the subject matter: are there any objects or words that dominate the dream? If there are, do you associate them with anything that may have acted as a trigger for that dream? Always remember dreams are not necessarily logical so you may have to try working through word associations, or seeing if one event could have a significant link to another.

Eventually you will see a pattern emerge and will be able to gain an insight into your inner self – as well as some of the events that influence your life. You also may well begin to understand when your dreams are highlighting a positive period in your life as well as recognising when those REM sleep activities are showing you that you are emotionally stressed and are having to cope with more pressure than is good for you.

The whole art of interpreting your dreams is understanding them in a way that makes them work for you. They may tell you something about yourself or the position that you're in at that particular time. They may help you identify a problem, or even solve one. Recurring dreams, in particular, can be caused by a consistent avoidance of dealing with troublesome emotions and attitudes: the dream may be repeated until the problem is out in the open and actually confronted.

Learning to understand your dreams is a little like acquiring a new skill: the more you practise the better you get. Also, the more you learn about the whole art of interpretation, the more interesting it becomes: suddenly you begin to make connections that hitherto had gone unrecognised.

It is also important to persevere. Like understanding a new language, your first attempts may well end in complete frustration. This is another reason why keeping a record of your dreams is such a good thing: as the weeks go on you are able to see just how much you've learnt, despite what you may actually feel at the time.

After a while, you should also find that you start to 'read' your own symbolism, or the images of the unconscious mind, and in many ways you're the best person to do so. After all, only you know whether, say, dreaming of the country is likely to represent a fondly remembered childhood or a bed of triggers for a chronic allergy that you've been trying to control for years.

Whatever you think of your dreams, and however you choose to interpret them, it's important to remember that it's up to you to get exactly what you want out of them. Dreaming should be seen as a positive experience and your dreams are there to be enjoyed as much as anything else. Dreaming is about making your dreams work for you. Once you start doing that, the only thing you need to do is lie there and enjoy them whenever possible.

We'll show you how to find the true meaning of your dreams and how you can make them work for you in chapter 8 on page 104. But first, we need to explore those dreams we never forget – nightmares!

6

nightmares,
night terrors and
lucid dreams

'*It was a real nightmare,*' we say all too often about some problem we've had to solve in our everyday life. But this obscures the main element of a genuine nightmare, which is the overwhelming sense of terror and powerlessness. In fact this sense of being threatened by some often unidentified horror is reflected in the origin of the word itself: *mare* is the Old English word for 'demon'!

Before we look at nightmares in detail, we need to distinguish between them and what are usually known as 'night terrors'. Although these are more common in children (see chapter 8), some people go on experiencing them all their adult life or at intervals. One survey found that they represented around 4 per cent of the total of what are generally referred to as nightmares.

According to Professor Arthur Crisp of St George's Hospital in London, around 5 per cent of adults suffer from this problem.

One of the main differences between the two is that, unlike nightmares, night terrors are not dreams in the true sense. They tend to occur during a phase of non-REM (or non-dreaming) sleep during the early part of the night, and are rarely accompanied by specific visual images. It seems that most terrors occur during the deepest phase of sleep – stage 4 – when brain activity as measured on an EEG in a sleep lab is at its slowest. Nightmares, on the other hand, are a feature of REM sleep, and usually occur in a later part of the night.

Waking up feeling absolutely scared to death is obviously horrifying for the victim of night terrors, but it can be equally alarming for anyone sharing the same bedroom or even the same house. Usually, the sleeper will sit bolt upright in bed, having previously been apparently sound asleep, and scream or cry out loudly. They will look as though their mind is somewhere else other than the bedroom, staring into space with wide eyes and looking scared out of their wits. Comforting the person isn't easy either, because they have no fantastic story to tell as with a nightmare. At most, there may be some fleeting remembered image, but no plot or visual images, however strange. The sensation of fear is very powerful, but will gradually fade – and be gone completely within half an hour or so. Strangely, if they can go back to sleep as soon as they have calmed down, they may have no memory of the incident at all the following morning.

Although one researcher found that night terrors could sometimes be set off by a sudden loud noise, this is obviously not the whole explanation.

The pattern of terrors

Sleep lab studies have shown that people who suffer from night terrors have a particular pattern of sleep – that is, they have a tendency to wake directly out of stage 4 sleep instead up coming back to consciousness gradually through the lighter stages. Sometimes, this pattern of waking may be repeated as many as five times a night, although there may well be no terror associated with some of the wakenings. Even so, a person whose sleep is regularly broken in this way can end up feeling very exhausted.

As well as having this special kind of sleep pattern, adults who suffer repeatedly from night terrors may be naturally anxious types says Professor Crisp, and will probably find that the problem gets worse when they are under particular strain for some reason in their daily lives. For the majority of sufferers, making a big effort to sort out and deal with this kind of stress will probably be enough to keep the attacks under control. In any case, it's important to remember that, frightening though they are, night terrors are not serious in themselves, and are not a symptom of any illness.

In rare cases, night terrors can lead to other problems or dangerous behaviour. Some examples include sleepwalking or, more rarely, menacing behaviour such as threatening other people in the same room or house or even hurting themselves accidentally, by putting their hand through a window, for instance. For the minority of people who experience these kinds of terrors, some form of help – such as psychotherapy – may be needed to sort out the difficulties which are causing the underlying stress.

Fears at bedtime

Nightmares are rather more common than terrors, and most of us will have had them at some time in our lives. One study found that around one in twenty of us has a nightmare at least once a week, but some people suffer from them more often, in certain cases every single night.

We recognise them not primarily from the visual images or the 'story', but by the emotions they invariably invoke: fear, horror and sometimes guilt. If you've recently seen a frightening film or read a thriller, you might replay scenes from the story in your dream, but provided the unpleasantness isn't directed at you or someone you love, you may be quite content to watch the developments passively and without any fear. So, while the visual and plot content may have something in common with a nightmare, you won't experience it as one unless the emotional content is appropriate. As in waking life, the sensation of terror is accompanied by a physical reaction. You wake up sweating and breathing hard, and you can feel your heart pounding.

So what is it that sets this horrible set of sensations off? First you need to eliminate purely physical causes. Most of us have heard the old wives' tale about not eating cheese just before bedtime because it will give us nightmares, and there is some truth in this. By no means all nightmares are caused by indigestion, but eating a heavy or rich meal late at night can be a factor on some occasions. Normally, the body slows down or stops many of its daytime physical operations while we sleep – including digestion. By forcing it to deal with a large meal, we can disturb the quality of our sleep, and it may be that the biochemical process involved in digestion triggers bad dreams. Some people have also suggested that feeling guilty about eating too much could provoke nightmares, but of course, whether you react in this way depends on how you feel about food.

Although there is little evidence that drinking a lot of alcohol causes nightmares, heavy drinkers who then stop drinking may have frightening dreams for some time afterwards. The same seems to be true of other drugs which affect the central nervous system, such as tranquillisers. This is important because the type of sleeping pills most often prescribed today are actually mild tranquillisers, and although they are far less dangerous than older barbiturate sleeping pills, they may cause side-effects when you stop taking them. All these substances have the effect of damping down the workings of the central nervous system, reducing the user's response to stress. Once you stop taking them, your system can respond with a powerful 'rebound' effect, increasing anxiety levels and so making bad dreams more likely. Doctors are increasingly aware of the possible side-effects of prescribing these types of drugs, and will often only dispense them in special circumstances and for relatively short periods. There are a number of other, non-drug approaches to tackling insomnia, and it is worth trying these rather than relying on sleeping pills if you possibly can.

The stuff of nightmares

While some people may recognise these 'pharmacological' factors as being the probable cause of their nightmares, they do not apply to the majority of us, whether we have recurring nightmares or just the occasional one. One of the strangest things about a nightmare is that you recognise it for what it is as soon as it begins. Many people say that they sometimes don't even know what it is that they are frightened of – the monster that is threatening them may not even appear but is more a lurking, unseen menace.

In this kind of nightmare, it is not the visual images which are the moving force, but the feeling of fear itself. The pictures may be relatively uninteresting or undramatic in themselves, but the interpretation your brain puts on them is the source of the horror. At other times, the terror seems to arise from what you see happening – you're faced by someone trying to attack you with a carving knife, or threatened by some frightening animal that's about to pounce on you, for example.

Being pursued by some kind of threat, whether human, animal or supernatural, is a feature of very many nightmares, and the terror usually arises from the dreamer's inability to escape. However hard you try, you can't seem to move fast enough to get away. The explanation for this is almost certainly the paralysis that is always present during REM sleep: at some level, your mind is aware that you cannot move, and this is reflected in the nightmare experience. Dr Keith Hearne suggests that the most effective way to deal with this kind of nightmare is simply to relax – once you give up the struggle to move, the nightmare will dissolve naturally into an ordinary and unfrightening dream. It may take a bit of practice, but it is certainly worth trying.

Some researchers have suggested that there may also be a physiological explanation which accounts, in part at least, for the overwhelming sensations of fear. The idea is that the electrical activity in the brain which continues while we sleep (see chapter 2) somehow activates primitive emotional circuits which control our most basic feelings and instincts, of which fear is one. This is especially likely to happen if we are in the grip of some anxiety or worry over something in our everyday life. This feeling is not suppressed during sleep, but instead helps to bring our more primitive emotions to the fore, generating frightening dreams.

Whether or not this is the correct explanation, there is a definite connection between our waking mood and nightmares. Worries and daily anxieties can prey on our minds at night, and especially just when we're trying to drop off to sleep. Dr Keith Hearne believes that the majority (96 per cent) of nightmares are simply anxiety dreams, and are usually preceded by more rapid breathing and an increased heart rate.

According to Professor Arthur Crisp, nightmares are likely to be related to a more generalised distress which is affecting the sleeper's daily life. Thus, the images and symbols we see in our nightmares will be influenced by what's going on in our ordinary lives.

Is this your nightmare?

Experts disagree about whether analysing the actual content of nightmares will shed any light on what is causing them. What they do tell you is that you are probably under some kind of stress or worrying consciously or unconsciously about a problem in your everyday life. The precise form your nightmare takes may not necessarily be related to the content of your dream, although it may well explain the feelings of fear and anxiety.

One study suggested that certain types of personality made

a person more prone to nightmares. The characteristics which appeared to increase a person's vulnerability were a tendency to be affected by feelings, apprehensiveness and a high level of tension.

One nightmare researcher compiled a list of the most common scenarios. According to Dr Keith Hearne, the chart-toppers are:

- Seeing a stranger being shot or suffering some other violence

- Being attacked or in danger yourself

- Trying to get away from someone or something

- Being aware of something or someone which is a threat, even if not actually visible

- Trying and failing to get somewhere on time

- Suffocation

- Paralysis

People who have at some time in their lives had to sit very important exams often say it is the most stressful experience they can remember. It is not surprising that many of them will have nightmares about being faced with an exam paper which makes no sense or knowing that something dreadful is going to happen because they've failed one. Common sense suggests that this kind of dream is likely to appear at a time when they feel under extreme pressure later in life, and it is more important to deal with that pressure than think too much about the nightmare itself.

While most experts would agree that nightmares are the result of stresses in our daily lives, some would go further and say that we can interpret the symbols and plots so as to pinpoint the problem. The usual approach is to help the sufferer to recognise that the 'madman with a knife', the 'bloodsucking monster', or whatever form the threat takes, is simply a reflection of the dreamer's own personality and self-perception.

For example, a vampire-like figure which holds you in an inescapable grip and sucks your blood could indicate that you feel that other people are demanding more from you than you feel able to give. Similarly, being threatened by a would-be killer might mean that there is some aspect of yourself or some recent action which makes you feel bad about about yourself. To use this method of analysis you would have to consider all aspects of your life and your personality, and try to work out what is causing the internal conflict being symbolically played out in your nightmare.

Dealing with a nightmare

Most modern therapists, however, agree that confrontation is the best way to deal with a nightmare, whether it's recurrent or a one-off. Whatever school of thought they belong to as to the importance and role of dreams, they agree that the solution is to turn and face the source of your terror. This sounds simple, but requires a certain amount of preparation. It depends on the principle of lucid dreaming – in other words, making yourself aware that you're dreaming while the experience is taking place. To do this, you start by giving yourself regular reminders during the day that you are awake and not asleep. Then, if you've been having nightmares, remind yourself last thing at night that you will not let the terror take over but will face up to it.

The idea is to keep somewhere in your mind the knowledge that this is a dream and the images causing your fear are all coming from inside your own head. Then when the nightmare begins, tell yourself you must tackle the threat head-on. Exactly what happens will depend on the form the dream takes, but if, for instance, you're being chased, you don't run but stand your ground and fight back.

Alternatively, if your attacker has the power of speech, you can ask why it's pursuing you, and what you've done to incur its aggression. Dreams being what they are, the precise consequences are unpredictable, but invariably the threat will dissolve and lose its power to terrify. Sometimes you may have to have several goes before you can remember what you're supposed to do, but the technique is very effective in the end.

People who have suffered from recurring nightmares to the point where it affected their everyday lives have benefited from hypnotherapy to enable them to control their night-time experiences. The therapist explains the technique of recognising a nightmare for what it is and confronting the threat directly. Dr Keith Hearne describes this as 'informational therapy', and points out that because you always know when a dream is a nightmare, you can learn to intervene in the plot at this point and ward off the unpleasantness. He recounts the case of one nightmare sufferer who was successfully treated by hypnosis, and told his therapist afterwards:

> I recalled what you said about controlling the dream when I recognised the scenery that usually precedes my nightmare. With a sudden illumination of dream lucidity, I decided to make the dream pleasant and soon found myself on a golden beach. I was very exhilarated.

So, for this man, recognising the setting in which the dream took place was the signal for him to intervene and turn a negative experience into a positive one.

Another sufferer recalled a similar experience:

> I was being chased by something – a real monster. I suddenly realised that this was a recurring nightmare and that I could control everything. I stopped, turned round and faced the creature. I said to it: 'I'm going to shrink you!' With that, the creature turned into a furry little animal that scurried away. I felt a marvellous sense of being in control.

There is obviously no doubt that many people have found this approach effective in dealing with nightmares, which raises an interesting question. If we can decide in advance to behave in a particular way within a nightmare, this implies that we can be aware that we are dreaming, and that we can then use this awareness to control our dreams, to some extent at least.

When you know it's a dream

While these implications raise all kinds of problems for those who believe that dreams are essentially junk with no meaning, it makes perfect sense to people who regularly have this kind of experience. Many people say that they have dreams in which they are, at some level, aware that they are dreaming. Some actually use this to cut short unpleasant dreams or ones which are turning nasty. They are able to say to themselves – I don't like this situation, I'm getting out of here – and simply wake themselves up. This awareness that 'it's only a dream' experienced while actually in the middle of the experience, is what experts call 'lucid dreaming'.

Unfortunately, it is difficult to find enough people who are able to do this – or think they can – to study in a scientific set-up. Because people who do experience lucid dreams don't perceive them as a problem in the way that nightmares and night terrors are, it's actually quite difficult to find a significant number of people to take part in research!

Also, the reality is that those studied may need to sleep in the lab for months before producing a lucid dream. Even then, it would be difficult to make any kind of measurements or carry out tests to confirm objectively what the dreamer says was happening. For, while a subject may report afterwards that they were having a lucid dream, it is difficult for the researchers to be aware of this while it is happening.

Some years ago, Dr Hearne tried various ways of communicating with a lucid dreamer during his dream. One method

73

involved an agreed code of eye movements by which the dreamer could signal to the researcher that he was having a lucid dream while it was happening. Some people managed to do this successfully, and their eye movements were recorded on the oculogram – the electronic measuring device which registers what's happening under a dreamer's closed eyelids.

The 'dream machine'

Another experiment attempted to induce lucid dreaming using a specially constructed 'dream machine'. The subjects were told that they would be given a tiny electric shock to their wrist at intervals during their dreams, and this was the signal to trigger awareness that they were dreaming. Once they became aware, they were to use deliberate eye movements to let the researcher know. Dr Hearne reported that while a few people could develop this awareness, it was much more difficult to use it to control their dreams.

Since doing his original research, Dr Hearne has developed and refined his machine, so that it can now be used as an aid to nightmare prevention as well as to induce lucid dreaming. The prototype of a machine which may soon be available commercially is currently under test. About the size of a small paperback, with sensors which are attached to the sleeper's body, the machine monitors his breathing. Just before we enter a phase of dreaming sleep, our breathing changes from being slow, steady and deep to becoming shallow, variable and rapid. The more stressed we are, the more dramatic this change. The machine can be adjusted so that the alarm gets louder when it senses changes that mean that the sleeper is under some sort of stress.

It can also be set to wake the person even during normal dreams, as a way of increasing dream recall. Unfortunately, as Dr Hearne points out, it can't yet tell when the dream is so good that the sleeper would prefer not to be woken!

Some people have also learned to have lucid dreams with the aid of the machine. They are taught to recognise that four electrical pulses to their wrist while they're sleeping are a signal to ask themselves whether they are dreaming. If the signal successfully triggers an awareness, they can then attempt to control the shape and content of the dream.

Learning to have lucid dreams could have practical uses, but it could also be a rather appealing way to enjoy yourself while you sleep. Psychologist Dr Susan Blackmore sees the technique both as a way of helping people to deal better with their problems and as a gateway to dream-time entertainment. First, however, you have to teach yourself to become aware that you're dreaming while you're doing it, and that isn't easy.

Three steps to lucid dreaming

Dr Blackmore suggests three ways for people to try that will help them to turn their dreams into lucid ones:

* First, ask yourself frequently whether you are dreaming. Do it whenever you remember all the time you're awake and especially just before you go to bed. The idea is to make the question a constant presence in your thoughts, so that it will eventually pop into your mind while you're actually dreaming.

* Second, before you fall asleep, tell yourself that you will have at least one dream that you'll remember, and that however real it may seem, it will still only be a dream.

* Third, set your alarm to wake you about an hour and a half after you've gone to sleep when you're likely to be mid-dream. When you wake up, concentrate on recalling your dream, then get up and walk about for a few minutes. When you get back into bed, read for a few minutes before you settle back to sleep, telling yourself as you do so that you will have another dream.

The idea behind all this is gradually to develop awareness that what seems so real while you're dreaming is no more than an illusion – the product of your mind's own creative talents. Once you have grasped this basic fact, it's obvious that your dream can therefore be controlled by your mind. Once you've managed this, theoretically you can take charge of events and turn them in whatever direction you choose.

The fun bit comes in when you decide to turn your dreams into the equivalent of waking fantasies – pleasant episodes where everything goes the way you want and you have a great time!

In principle, if you can control the content of your dreams, there should be no reason why you shouldn't take the opportunity to tackle practical or theoretical problems which you haven't managed to resolve in the normal way. There have been many stories recorded of this kind of thing happening, the most famous of which is how the chemist Kekule found the chemical structure of benzene.

He knew the chemical composition of the benzene molecule, and that it consisted of six atoms of hydrogen and six of carbon, but he had been unable to find a way of linking them to form a model which satisfied the basic laws of chemistry.

One night he fell asleep in front of the fire while thinking about his problem, and dreamt of six snakes writhing about. Suddenly, one of them took hold of its own tail in its mouth and the chemist immediately woke with the conviction that he had solved his problem. He based his model of benzene on a ring rather than the conventional chain – and so found the answer.

It sounds like a marvellous way of overcoming obstacles, but the problem is that there is very little evidence that this desirable technique is available to the rest of us. A psychologist at the University of Swansea who has investigated this and other similar stories, points out that while the content of our dreams often relates to daily life, our ability to think and reason logically in dreams appears to be limited.

We also seem to lack any imagination, says researcher Allan Rechtschaffen, in the sense that we can't let our minds wander but must concentrate on the events unrolling before our startled gaze. We can't turn away and think of something else, nor can we analyse what's happening or reflect on it.

Perhaps what we may be able to do sometimes is to make connections or associations between things which would not occur to our rational, waking minds simply because they don't seem to make any sense. If people do manage to get insight into theoretical problems in their dreams, it's conceivable that it could be through this kind of lateral thinking. When logic and reason don't seem to be much help to us in our daily lives, why not turn instead to the supremely illogical and irrational world of dreams for an alternative approach to the problems facing us? It's certainly worth giving it a try.

7

children and dreams

Talk to any child about their dreams and the chances are you'll get one of two stories. It'll either be an action-packed tale of swashbuckling heroics, where good rules over evil and no one goes without, or you may hear haunting stories of a world full of monsters, all larger than life and each and every one out to get the dreamer.

And such is the stuff of our children's dreams, you may say. But is it? Could it be more likely that such vivid pictures are nothing to do with sleep – they're simply the work of an active imagination? With children, in their waking world as well as their dream world, nothing is necessarily what it seems.

As we've already seen, in one form or another, dreams reflect our reality and our minds have the ability to switch from a waking world to a dream world and to decide – unconsciously, illogic-ally or otherwise – which parts of the reality to reflect. And as a child's world and experiences are often very different from an adult's, it follows that their dreams have a different 'flavour' and may, therefore, take on an altogether different meaning.

Unlike adults, children are still laying down experiences and attempting to interpret the world around them. They are still trying to work things out – all of which is reflected in their world of dreams. In fact, even though they may be exposed to the same experiences as us, how they interpret them is determined by what they understand about the world and their relationships within it, as well as with each other. And this is clearly seen in their dreams.

Baby talk

Without doubt, there is a strong link between dreaming and development: in fact experts have managed to establish that even babies who are still in the womb will experience REM sleep! Ultrasound scans have revealed that REM sleep can occur as early as twenty-three weeks into a pregnancy, although you may wonder how anyone can determine anything to do with the thoughts and dreams of an unborn child.

However, scientists have been able to observe the existence of REM sleep in babies in the same way as they monitor it in adults: which is that during a 'dream sequence' the eyeball moves around rapidly. So, as soon as the foetus' eyelids develop, scientists are in a position to measure the amount of movement.

Furthermore, research carried out some years ago discovered that dreaming was more frequent in the last three months of pregnancy. This, presumably, may have something to do with the fact that during the last trimester, the brain is developing at least as fast as the rest of the body. In fact, it seems that the REM sleep of the unborn child is as much a part of its development as is thumb-sucking and the transformation of 'webbed' feet into separate toes.

Once a baby is born, while it is still impossible to do more than speculate what images and concerns are filling their REM sleep, experts and non-experts alike are at least in a position to observe. And as any new parent knows only too well, part of the joy of watching a sleeping baby is noticing, every so often, the grunts, the smacking of lips, the clenching of fists and the deep sighs which appear to be the result of utter contentment, as well as a signal that the baby has just entered a particularly energetic period of REM sleep!

For the first two weeks of a baby's life, 50 per cent of the time asleep will be taken up with dreams. By the time he's a year old, dreaming takes up about five hours of each day but as a child grows, REM sleep makes up less of their sleep time and the amount continues to fall until we're about 18. By then, the amount of REM sleep falls into the adult pattern of forming just a quarter of total sleep.

The developing dream world

In fact the type of dreams children have largely follow a developmental sequence in the same way that, say, their level of coordination or motor skills develop. So, young children will dream of an inner world which is represented by their family and events like shopping, playing and parties – things that affect them directly. An older child will dream of their relationships in an outside world – anything from something they've read in the paper to an event they've learnt about at school – happenings which obviously go way beyond their immediate reality. So, as you might expect, their dreams will reflect these influences depending on the stage they are going through.

A dream can also tell us a lot about a child's age: a 4-year-old might dream of his teddy, for instance, whilst a 12-year-old's dream may be inspired by a conflict with a teacher at school. And the older the children are, often the more complex their dreams become as their world view gets wider and more involved. All these developments mean their relationships are more sophisticated and their subconscious more highly developed.

Age also imposes language restrictions on the child's ability to describe his dreams – the younger they are, the less likely they are to be able to express themselves in anything more than simplistic terms. One study revealed that when a group of 3–5-year-olds were asked to relay their dreams, their descriptions amounted to 14 words on average. However, by the time children had reached the 9–11 age group their descriptions had expanded: girls used around 75 words, boys about 60. The maximum number of words used was 443 for girls and 249 for boys. So, the more sophisticated their language and experience becomes, the more words they are able to use to describe their dreams.

In fact, American dream expert Patricia Garfield also discovered that a female's descriptions are longer because they not only remember more of their dreams, but they also use more words: 'Adjectives and detailed descriptions are far more frequently employed by women in writing and speaking . . . probably due to their superior skill in language. On average,' she explains, 'women test as more verbally fluent than men.'

The fear of fantasy

As we grow older, as well as our language developing, so does our use of symbolism and images in our dreams. Very young children rarely use symbolism which, logically, should mean that their dreams are fairly simple to understand. However, although a youngster may not dream in very sophisticated images, trying to interpret their dreams is made complicated by the fact that the younger the child, the more difficulty he will have distinguishing between fantasy and reality. So, before you even sit down and start to make sense of your child's 'story', you have first to determine where the dream world ends and imaginative play begins.

For example, if a young child wakes up in the dark, still of the night and perceives a shadow as a monster, he may well slip back into sleep and dream of that monster. Conversely, if he was dreaming of monsters and then wakes up and notices a large shadow on the wall, it's easy for that shadow to metamorphose into some giant, threatening monster. For children the dark masks a world of hidden dangers that can take the form of either fantasy figures or real figures, or both. However, whatever form they take, these figures have one thing in common: they have the power to appear only when everyone else is asleep.

A young child's fear of the dark is something many parents know only too well but that fear can manifest itself in many ways. One mother tells the story of her son, standing by the bed, night after night, deeply distressed because whenever he dropped off to sleep 'the dreams kept coming'.

To ask a young child to distinguish between dreaming and reality is asking a lot: on the one hand those dreams reflect the 'real world' that surrounds them (family, familiar settings, the park, animals and so on) whilst, on the other hand, these images take on a life of their own as fantasy replaces reality. Understandably the child can become scared of their nightly mental creations.

What's more, unlike a grown-up, the child's mind knows no restrictions – his fantasies aren't limited by practicalities such as distance, or money or skill. Theirs is the world where everyone gets to be friends with Mickey Mouse and anyone can be a train driver. Equally, wicked witches can fly and nasty men can turn boys into donkeys – just like they did in *Pinnochio*.

In many ways reality is essentially an adult concept and for a child the line where reality ends and fantasy begins is blurred. And while we understand that shadows can't turn into animals and that teddies don't talk, in the child's mind they do. After all, how easy is it to distinguish fantasy from reality in a world where talking mice, like Mickey and Minnie Mouse, and wicked witches are recognised as images of good and evil by millions of children?

It's easy to understand that life is a confusing experience for children and we need to show that we appreciate some of the fears that our children are trying to confront. As one psychiatrist explains, 'If you went to sleep one night and found a tiger in your bed, would you want to go back?' In fact, even though the child doesn't think of the tiger as actually in the bed before he goes to sleep, 'the child knows that when he closes his eyes it may return to pounce upon him.'

What, of course, makes it worse for a young child in particular is that his grasp of language is not sophisticated enough to convey the vividness of the fantasy – or the fear that he attaches to it. And even though he may not be able to express the depth of his feelings, it doesn't take anything away from the fact that his feelings towards sleep are coloured by his experience as much as by his family's response to that experience.

Fact or fiction?

Some psychologists have argued that looking too deeply into the dreams of our children has limited value. And while a dream that tells the story of monsters or goblins springs from the child's fantasy land, not all dreams are quite so dramatic. Way back in the 1920s, one dream expert, a Dr Kimmins, discovered that it was common for children up to the age of about 7 to confuse dreaming with waking. So, if they dreamt they'd lost a toy, they might wake up and immediately start frantically looking for it; or they may dream that a parent had gone away, and then be surprised to find that same parent happily tucked up in bed the next morning as usual.

Even more fascinating was a piece of American research that explored the same idea, but in more clinical conditions. One study, which was carried out in a sleep laboratory, involved waking a young boy up, moments after he had shown signs of obvious REM activity. When the child was questioned about whether he had been dreaming, he insisted that he hadn't. Although the research was repeated several times, the answer was always the same. Needless to say, this confounded the researcher – until he decided to use a different approach. The next time the boy was woken up, instead of asking him whether he'd dreamt he said, 'What were you doing just now?' The different phrasing of the same question resulted in a completely different response: 'Oh, I was just playing with a tyre on the back porch . . .'

Obviously it must be hard initially for children to determine the difference between the outside world of reality and the inner world of dreams and it's easy to understand why many youngsters like 4-year-old Sam talk about 'pictures in my head' as if this were as normal as thinking about food at dinner time. In fact, one 5-year-old, when asked how he knows when he's dreaming, offered a simple explanation that, he claims, always helps him tell the difference: 'When I pinch myself, if it doesn't hurt it means I'm dreaming; if it does hurt it means I'm not dreaming'!

Why children dream

We've already seen in chapter 2 why people dream and for children the explanations can be equally complex. There is no one simple answer or explanation for their dreams, any more than there is for ours. Certainly the dominant view these days is that the role they play can be attributed to a number of things – depending on the child and depending on the circumstances. In her excellent book, *Children Dreaming* (Penguin, 1989), counsellor Brenda Mallon discusses how, for our children, dreams have a vital and unique role. She describes five possible explanations, many of which echo the theories that surround the meaning of adult dreams.

* They can help sort out the events of the day: this is the 'Computer Theory', first put forward by psychologist Christopher Evans, by which dreams are seen as echoing daily

events and assimilating them; they help us sort out what's gone on in the preceding 24 hours.

- They act as a vehicle for wish-fulfilment: they offer escapism – whether from unhappiness or boredom, and they allow the child to live out his greatest fantasies. For children that may mean anything from visiting Sesame Street to going out with their favourite pop star.

- They help prepare us for a future event and therefore anticipate possible scenarios: for a child that could mean dreaming of being a bridesmaid or pageboy – or even starting a new school.

- They can also help sort out problems as they allow a child to reflect and, in some cases, even resolve problems, albeit on a relatively simple level.

- They help us communicate: Mallon notes that, with children as well as adults, dreams are used in therapy, 'because they communicate unconscious conflicts, anxieties and fears'. So, we may dream of something that acts as a message to ourselves.

It's easy to see that for children as well as adults, dreams are undoubtedly influenced by their present circumstances. But, when it comes to the actual content, what exactly is the stuff of our children's dreams?

For most children, the majority of their dreams centre around play and make-believe, although it's been shown that the child who has a higher rate of unpleasant and disturbing dreams is more likely to have some emotional or psychological problem.

Obviously there is a lot of 'cross-fertilisation' between real events that take place during the day and dreamed events that occur at night and, for a child, a dream is as much a way of exploring all the elements that make up his waking experience as it is a way of making sense of it. So, children's dreams don't simply reflect their reality, or lives, they also reveal exactly what they understand about reality. Fantasy, like play, is a serious business for a child and the way their fantasy world unfolds – whether it's in their dream world or real world – can tell you as much about them as it can about their dreams.

The material, or if you prefer, the events that are played out in their dream world, will also reveal something about the sort of characters and people – the reality – that is uppermost in the child's mind. However, the context in which those events take place (in other words, how these characters are depicted, the emotions and scenes that occur) will tell you about the child himself and how he is emotionally perceiving, as well as coping with, his life.

And how they dream

Of course dreams also represent and express important concerns that the child has about himself. That includes his fears as well as his wishes and worries. However, what's interesting is that so many children, through their dreams, express these feelings by dreaming of animals. One psychologist believes this is because for children, adults play distinctive roles – anything from protector to punisher. So, they can only be defined in a way that children are familiar with. What's more, the position they have in the child's life is clearly defined – regardless of whether that position is one of an authority-figure, nurturer, guide, or even killjoy!

What all this role-modelling means is that for children, grown-ups can never assume the guise of a fantasy figure. For the child they're just too closely identified as a grown-up who acts in a grown-up way, and no amount of dressing up as Father Christmas – or anything else for that matter – can change that. However, the same is not true of animals. Animals can, and do, assume fantasy roles in all of our children's lives, which probably goes some way to explaining why they are such a successful vehicle for a child's fantasy world.

For proof, look no further than children's literature, films or cartoon characters. Most children are familiar with wise owls, sneaky snakes and mischievous monkeys. And the beauty of animals is that they can be, and often are, anything that the child wants them to be.

Animals are also very much involved in all aspects of play – and therefore fantasy – in a child's life from a very early age. And if you need any further proof of this, just count up the number of cuddly toys that the average preschooler possesses! Consequently, it is relatively easy for animals to take on a fantasy role in the child's dream world.

The early years

A young child's experiences and interests tend to be narrow and generally revolve around the familiar, for example, the home and family. Obviously family members loom large and if both parents work, childcarers will equally find a place in that child's dreams along with animals and fantasy figures.

The short accounts of dreams given by 3- and 4-year-olds generally contain little action or emotion – their dreams are simply full of the familiar. However, the accounts produced by children a couple of years older are not only longer but also involve more activity. Interestingly in both cases the dreamer tends to play a passive role.

But differences aren't just down to age. It seems that gender plays a part too. Girls apparently dream more of pleasant feelings, enjoyable encounters and generally 'happy endings'. Boys on the other hand seem to dream more of conflicts and negative situations. However, research has shown that by the time children reach the ages of 7 and 8, these differences are no longer noticeable. Of course much of this evidence may be down to early role models and our 'expected' behaviour.

If girls are taught that they should behave differently from boys, and their early influences have consciously been feminine (dolls, tea sets, jewellery and 'mini mum' type toys) then their dreams are likely to reflect this. Our female role models are based on the women in our lives which, for a toddler, may be limited to Mum and Grandma.

It's only as we get older that we become aware that there are alternatives to the roles that we are exposed to when we're young. The same is obviously true for young boys when normal high spirits are deemed to be innate and therefore acceptable – a label that only serves to reinforce the myth that little girls are made of 'sugar and spice and all things nice', whereas little boys are relegated to the stuff of 'slugs and snails and puppy dog tails'!

Interestingly, while boys may dream of being chased by giants and gorillas, girls are more likely to dream of witches. Witches, incidentally, are thought to be a fairly common representation of a mother in a dream world – particularly when a girl has recently had a row with her mum and is still smarting at the memory!

Many dreams which children of this age group have revolve around goodies and baddies, which is probably as much due to visual (TV, videos) as well as literary influences. Watch almost any children's cartoon and you can't help but be struck by the predictability of them all. The themes rarely differ: good versus bad; struggles ensue until eventually – against all odds – good wins through. If you like, it's simply Superman by another name. Children understand reality in similar terms; they have yet to develop the sophistication to understand events on a more complex level.

As the child gets older his dreams become more complex and symbols begin to represent people as well as objects. So, parents may become any sort of figure of authority, small animals may represent younger sisters or brothers and houses may represent people generally.

The School Years
The dreams of those early school days are similar to pre-school in as much as fact mixes with fantasy while good continues to

grapple with evil. Ghosts, monsters and animals figure heavily as do the heroes and villains of the day. Dreams where the child feels anxious are fairly common and this can become particularly acute when a child is starting, or changing, school. This is hardly surprising when you think that a change of school – a major new environment in their life – is likely to plunge even the most confident child into a world of uncertainty where their identity is yet to be established. Suddenly they have new faces to recognise, new rules to learn and a hitherto unknown framework to fit into. No wonder that the whole experience can cause wakeful nights and stressful dreams.

The child needs to share his worries and discover that it's all right to feel nervous and all right to be confused. As the child becomes more settled in school and starts to establish it in his own mind as his territory, almost as much as home, the dreams should start to diminish. However, if he constantly has unpleasant dreams, parents should discuss it with his teacher. It's obviously vital that he or she is alerted to what your child is feeling. Most important though, never ignore your child's dreams if they are disturbing enough to bother him seriously. In young children, particularly, dreams may be the only means they have to give real expression to what they're experiencing.

Patricia Garfield notes that starting school can stir up a whole host of emotions in the child and that these can easily result in bad dreams such as 'being chased and attacked or of being injured or killed'. In fact her research revealed that the peak of nightmares for children is around the 5–7 age group, when the child is more likely to be experiencing the new and more stressful environment of school. What's more, teachers and classmates who cause fear or admiration can become part of the child's dreams.

Happier dreams for children can reveal their fantasies. So a little girl may see herself as a princess: a symbol of perfection and an image of someone who looks best, behaves best, is liked best and can have whatever she wishes. Boys may take on a

Thunderbirds role – once again helping good grapple with evil. These sorts of dreams give an insight into the activities within a child's world as well as the wishes and perception of reality.

Families can be the centre of as much conflict as comfort and many children experience dreams that reflect this confusion. An overpowering monster can be a representation of an overpowering parent or a situation where the child has been frightened by a parent or some other authority-figure. An argument at home can result in the offending person being turned into a force of evil – and then getting their come-uppance. Guilt is also represented in dreams: particularly when a child has done something that they know will cause disapproval – so much so that they are keeping quiet and hoping no one will find out!

As children get older their dreams become increasingly related to events in the real world and less to fantasy-figures – although fantasy still plays a part in their life, particularly when it is linked to wish-fulfilment. However, a sad reflection of our times is that children's dreams relating to fears are frighteningly focused. During her research, Brenda Fallon noticed a preponderance of dreams amongst the 6–10 age group that reflected a very real fear of feeling unprotected and unsafe. And, when she referred back to past studies to see if this was a part of the dreamer's developmental process she found that there were no records of dreams relating to such events as, say, kidnapping.

Fears will also depend on a child's individual situation. If they know of someone who has had a bad car accident, understandably one dream may be that they, or a close relative, could suffer the same fate. And a child in a war-torn community is likely to have different dreams from a child who lives in the relative security of the Home Counties. Some fears may be more abstract. Surveys have revealed that many children are increasingly concerned about the ozone layer, as well as the threat of nuclear warfare. All these concerns may be reflected in dreams – either directly or through people or fantasy characters that take on a symbolic stance that signifies power or control.

Older children

School looms large for the older child and this is reflected in their dreams. Exams, pressure of work, keeping up with your peers, failing – all can be represented in the older child's dreams. Added to this, the child's inner, as well as outer, reality is changing. Puberty and adolescence can be a daunting time.

Teenagers have to cope with a changing body which causes havoc for their hormones and results in great waves of emotional turmoil. The period is often marked by an increased conflict with parents and, for some teenagers, almost anyone in authority. Sexual awareness develops – as does an interest in the opposite sex. In some cases the teenager may even have a body of an adult but still think like a child. They have to renegotiate their reality in terms of their relationships as well as the world in which they live.

Interestingly, one cross-cultural study of children spanning six countries revealed that certain themes rated highly when it came to the children's concerns. These included fear of not achieving well in school, being suspected of lying, poor school reports and being sent to the Head.

Understandably, as the child becomes an adolescent, dreams may involve separation from the family or concern situations where they find themselves alone. Such dreams may reflect the adolescents' anxiety about 'growing up' and all that this entails. It can also be a way of preparing themselves for such inevitabilities, particularly if they are going on to higher education which means that they are likely to leave home.

For girls, dreams can be particularly vivid – notably around the time of their period. Patricia Garfield believes that the hormonal upheaval in a young woman's body as she reaches menarche appears symbolically – blood and woundings being strong, and often dominant, images. Sexual encounters also play a part in dreams. For girls her research has revealed that, 'Early sexual episodes often produce pain and guilt leading to dreams of houses being broken into, damaged goods, or soiled bridal dresses.'

If the girl's experience was brutal then nightmares are likely to occur. 'She may dream of dismemberment, choking, being paralysed or crushed,' says Garfield. However, she discovered that if the girl's first experiences were loving 'the girl is more likely to dream of heroic males, romance, flowers and delicious foods.'

Interestingly, boys' dreams on the subject tend to be somewhat less romantic and are often much more specific in terms of the mechanics of sex! Adolescent boys have twice as many aggressive dreams as adolescent girls – although this may be more to do with the macho male role models we offer up in society than with any innate aggression on the part of the boy.

Other common dreams for this age group are a vast array of anxiety dreams. Brenda Fallon gives the example of one teenager who dreamt her teeth were falling out. This, she says, 'usually reflects feelings of insecurity about looks and separation, "falling out" with friends and relatives'. Being chased is another common dream for this age group. Experts see this as a positive sign as the dream tells of the dreamer's sense of frustration at not making progress. Progress is often not easy and, as Brenda Mallon points out, anxieties surface in dreams of this type.

Most people are familiar with dreams connected with falling, and this is a common theme in children's dreams too. As with adults' dreams, these are likely to reflect the child's feelings of being out of control or even the need to let go.

TV or not TV?

Clearly significant events in a child's life will influence their dreams – divorce, death, accidents. However, events unrelated to the family can also have considerable bearing on a child's dreams and those are the events which take place on television – even during so-called children's television.

Horror stories, and particularly those relating to children, are splashed across the papers and into our homes via television screens. The six o'clock news can be as disturbingly vivid as the nine o'clock bulletin, with little account taken of the effect that such exposure may have on young minds. Violence towards children, for example, horrifies the whole community, with parents everywhere being fearful for their children. But if the media can cause such a response in parents, one can only suppose the depth of effect that such coverage can have on children. There is no doubt that the media must play a part in defining the reality of our children's dreams if only because it plays such an integral part in their lives.

Child expert Dr Benjamin Spock believes frightening television programmes, especially in the evening, 'stir up and intensify the child's underlying fears'. It's his strong belief that violent and upsetting programmes are bad for children, whether or not the child shows anxiety. Even cruel fairy stories, he feels, should be avoided – particularly as the content has shown signs of seeping into the child's fantasy world at night.

Dr Spock is not alone in his advice and a quick glance at the current state of research can easily explain why. Brenda Mallon discovered that the vast majority of children dreamt about television characters and plots, 'though ages 8 and 14 showed peaks in which 84 per cent reported television inspired dreams.' What's particularly disturbing is that most were frightening dreams and nightmares. She also discovered that when disturbing films are seen by the child before sleep, there is a greater proportion of anxiety elements in the dreams during the REM sleep.

In fact, it seems that a child doesn't need to have actually seen a particularly violent or aggressive programme to have their dreams influenced by it. Children often discuss TV programmes, and 'cult' videos in particular, at great length with their friends, and in vivid detail. The 'pictures' created are so strong that the image stays with the child – regardless of whether they have seen that image firsthand.

However, it isn't only the obviously violent programmes that can significantly influence our children's dreams. One child that

Brenda Mallon talked to relayed a terrifying dream that was sparked off after watching an episode of a wildlife programme. So, seemingly innocent programmes can impinge on our sub-conscious. Essentially, in the majority of cases, the visual media (TV, video and film) encourage a passive relationship: the child need do no more than sit there while he soaks in the images that appear before him.

Books, on the other hand, involve a different sort of process. They allow a child some flexibility over what, and how, they digest the material. When parents read to younger children, they can edit out the scary bits or at least interrupt and explain in a way that is more palatable for a child. And older children have the option of putting a book down – or even skipping sections they find worrying. Also as reading levels limit the books a young person can read, generally the more disturbing stories contain complex language, as well as ideas, that they are unable to cope with, which means they're unlikely to be exposed to them.

For parents then, the key is being able to distinguish between the negative and positive media influences – as you can see later on in the chapter.

Nightmares

Despite any contribution that may be made by modern media, it's worth remembering that nightmares are nothing new and research carried out earlier this century showed that a quarter of all reported dreams were considered frightening. In the majority of these, the frightening image was that of an old man.

Nevertheless, there is no doubt that nightmares are more common when a child is anxious or worried. Recurrent ones indicate a basic insecurity – maybe at home or at school. Nightmares are also more frequent among children who are separated from their mothers, particularly if they have to go into hospital and so they are away from their own home and bed.

And the longer the period of separation, the more likely it is that nightmares will occur.

As we've already seen, disturbing dreams are not uncommon in children, particularly those between the ages of 4 and 6, although some American research has shown that at least a quarter of children between 6 and 12 still have bad dreams, many of which revolve around characters who reflect good and evil. We're all familiar with a child's delaying tactics come bedtime but for some youngsters this is an expression of a very real fear of the dark as well as a fear of monsters. To a child, their dreams can never be explained away as simply figments of their imagination.

As with adult dreams, the situation that the child finds himself in while dreaming tells us more about the child himself than the actual content which, to a certain extent, just uses characters and familiar situations as a 'language' by which he can express his fears. Both Freud and Jung, as well as present-day analysts, stressed the importance of the individual when trying to interpret a dream and in some ways their philosophy is even more relevant when discussing children who are unable to articulate their thoughts and feelings in the same way as adults. So, if a child dreams of being pursued by monsters, Gummi Bears or even Captain Hook, it's how they cope within the scene that reveals whether or not they are going through a period of feeling strong or feeling powerless.

It's usually around the age of 3 that nightmares can suddenly start to play a part in a child's 'nightlife'. This could be because this is the age at which children start to discover that their world is neither as safe, nor as certain, as they unquestionably believed in their first years. They have suddenly become aware of strangers, or new environments and even new stimuli in terms of cartoons and fantasy characters.

A child's nightmare also differs in power from an adult's. Sometimes, without even waking, a terrified youngster will continue screaming for his mother although she's crouched on the floor next to him, offering constant words of comfort and assurance. Research has also shown that young children in particular also have very detailed dreams, and are able to recall facial features accurately as well as specific objects such as furniture and toys.

Nightmares can also be a way for a child to express stress – particularly as young children are often unable to articulate their feelings and worries through language. It's important for parents not to ignore or make light of these vivid and distressing dreams and to check that there is no simple action they can take which will reduce the risk of the child suffering needlessly. On the following pages there is a checklist for parents plus guidance concerning what to do.

Sometimes a child's nightmares can have very simple explanations. Paediatricians have found that colds and nasal congestion can lead to bad dreams, particularly of drowning or suffocating, as can any illness where temperatures are raised. Dr Spock, on the other hand, has pointed to a number of more complex causes. For example, he believes that some nightmares may be due partly to, 'the normal guilt that children feel about being rivalrous with the parent of the opposite sex'.

Another explanation, for Spock, is that 'this is the age where children may struggle to understand the difference between sleep and death as well as understand the concept of death.' The confusion between the two, and uncertainty about what death is, can come to the surface during sleep as a nightmare. That said, though, according to Spock, the commonest cause of nightmares is frightening TV programmes and overexcited play.

How to help

Whatever theory you personally empathise with, one thing all the experts agree is that nightmares may often be stress-related and it can be hugely reassuring to your child to have you discussing his fears with him. It's important not to dismss his bad dreams or indeed make him feel guilty in any way. Try to find out whether anything is worrying him; maybe there's a problem at school, or an unresolved conflict with a friend. Also bear in mind the part that the family may play. While we may expect a critical life-event like a divorce to affect a child, even minor disagreements on the home front may have an effect on a sensitive child.

Remember, too, that a dream may often be triggered by an event that has taken place in the last twenty-four hours, so if your child does have a nightmare it's worth going over the day's events – including the day's viewing.

What you should do if your child wakes from a nightmare

At night:

- Most experts agree the first thing they need is reassurance. However much time you're prepared to spend discussing the problem, to a small child in the middle of the night, there's no substitute for the comfort that a cuddle can bring.

- Let them talk a little about the nightmare if they want to, but be careful not to force them to if they don't.

- Try to explain that the dream was just a story that they made up in their head while they were asleep.

- A really distressed child may be happier if you take them with you into a well-lit room, so that they wake enough to realise that despite the dream, everything is as it always is, and the familiar security of home hasn't changed because of a frightening dream.

- If the child refuses to be comforted, try talking about something in their lives that they are looking forward to – a party, a visit to friends – whatever might take their mind off the dream.

- Once they're reassured, stay with them until they get sleepy and can cope with being alone again. If they are still awake when you go, be sure to say you're going back to your room – don't just disappear, particularly if you think it will upset them all over again.

- Although parents may not want to set a precedent by inviting their child into their bed, the reassurance of having a grown-up nearby can often offer comfort that no words can. Interestingly, one piece of research revealed that children who don't sleep alone, and share their room (say, with a sibling) have fewer unpleasant dreams.

Ultimately the aim is to settle the child so he can go back to sleep. So, if you can, keep discussions about the nightmare down to a minimum. Ideally, leave discussion until the next morning when the cool light of day will enable the child to feel generally less emotional about the event.

The next day:

- Don't be surprised if your child doesn't actually remember the traumas of the night before. The powers of recall the morning after can often be fragmented, if they exist at all.

- If they do remember, try to provoke gentle conversation, emphasising again that the dream isn't real – and therefore it's nothing to be frightened of.

- Don't force a discussion – if they say they don't want to talk about it, it's important to respect that.

- Listen carefully to what's being said and see whether the tale rings any warning bells – maybe there's a dominant authority-figure (could it be a teacher?) who's pressurising the child; or their dream centres around getting to school late or not being told what's happening. Maybe the dream is just a reflection of the pressure that your child feels under.

- A dream is often triggered by events that have taken place in the preceding twenty-four hours, so it's always worth going over what happened the day before.

- Try to help the child to make sense of it – if it's possible. If there has been a direct cause of the nightmare, like a film or a video, try to explain the link in a way the child can understand.

- If the dream is a one-off, treat it that way and don't attach unnecessary long-term importance to it.

- If the dream is clearly based on a recurring theme, as with adult dreams, it probably means that the problem or concern is still bothering the child. What's more, the dreams are more likely to go on recurring until it is dealt with.

If you can't get to the bottom of your child's recurring nightmare, a little detective work may be in order. Talk to the child's friends, teachers – anyone who can shed light on why they are experiencing such disturbed nights. Dr Spock believes that if the child is generally well adjusted and isn't showing signs of problems and worries either at school, socially, or anywhere else that is significant in their life, then it may be best to adopt a wait-and-see approach as the problem could disappear as the child matures. Also, the older he gets, the more able he is to separate reality from fantasy as well as dreams from reality. As this happens, the child begins to make sense of his world and should, in turn, find the whole process less daunting.

However, if your child does keep having vivid, disturbing and recurring nightmares and you find you're unable to understand why, it's worth having a word with your doctor. The dreams could be an indication of a problem that needs attention and sometimes it can be easier for a dispassionate expert to deal with it than an emotionally involved parent.

What's more, however much you may question the necessity of involving the professionals, whichever way you look at it, doctors have generally had a lot more experience of dealing with sleep disorders than the rest of us, which means they have much more experience of ways to treat the problems, too. Repeated nightmares in particular should never be ignored. They may well be a sign that something is seriously wrong and it is important that, particularly if it is dominating your child's life, you seek professional help.

Brenda Mallon stresses the need to listen as well as respecting your child's dreams – good and bad. While you may sympathise with a dream triggered by a fear of a disabling accident, it's equally important that you show the same level of understanding when the fear centres on, say, an escaped monster or a spider that grows to huge, terrifying proportions. If the child has been disturbed enough to have a nightmare about something, then that should be taken as a signal of how important that issue is to that child.

It's also worth remembering that while we may well repress a traumatic event during our waking hours, we do not possess that sort of control over what happens when we sleep. And a nightmare may well be the way that our mind has of dealing with repressed events. Dreams can't be repressed. In fact in cases of child sexual abuse, one of the highest indicators of that abuse is the level of disturbance in dreams.

Dreams can form an important part of a child's life and whether the dream world is full of fun and fantasy or confusion and fear, the least we as grown-ups can do is listen and take notice, and let our children know that if their dreams are important to them, then they're important to us too.

'There is no culture of talking about dreams in this country,' says Brenda Mallon. 'Children, as well as adults, tend not to mention their dreams because they feel they are concerned with trivia. But dreams are important and can give clues to a child's emotional and psychological state.'

If the dream is important to a child, that's a good enough reason for it to be important to us. Acknowledging their dreams, as with everything in their lives, is a way of enhancing their self-esteem and giving them a sense of identity.

A word about night terrors

Terrors are most common in children in the 3–6 age group, although teenagers and even some adults can suffer from them. Although not that common, they are still thought to affect up to 5 per cent of children.

What happens

A night terror can result in a screaming, frightened child. He may sit bolt upright with eyes open, or even be moving around, clearly in a distressed state, screaming uncontrollably, convinced that he can see something frightening. Although he may seem awake, he is still totally taken up with the sensation of fear and it can be very difficult to get his attention away from it and back on to you and the 'real' world so you can comfort him. He may scream and shout, and even be uncharacteristically aggressive. This is all part of the 'terror' and quite normal – although normal is probably the last thing it seems at the time. The actual terror can last anything from ten minutes to the best part of an hour. Interestingly, in the vast majority of cases, the child remembers nothing of the event the next morning – and may even wonder why he's greeted by a heavy-eyed, overly concerned parent.

What you should do

Basically it all comes down to offering comfort, making sure the child doesn't hurt himself and being there when the terror has passed and he starts to come to. The terror has to take its course – although apparently switching on the lights may help bring it to a premature end. After the child has woken from the terror, it may take a while to calm him down. Once he has been re-assured and is calm, he's likely to go straight back to sleep.

Why do they happen

Although no one is certain, some experts believe terrors are caused by a 'fault' in the slow-wave sleep pattern – terrors always occur during the deepest stage of sleep.

Dr Bryan Lask, from London's Great Ormond Street Hospital, has said that:

> *Sleep is far deeper during the early part of the night, which is why the terrors tend to occur then, usually two to three hours after the child has fallen asleep. Some doctors say that part of the brain wakes while the rest remains asleep. The part that is awake is the part that affects the child's emotions. The part that is asleep controls the memory, which is why he doesn't remember anything about the episode the following day.*

Although, to the onlooker, a terror may seem like the be-haviour of a disturbed child, rest assured there is absolutely no evidence to suggest this. Furthermore, however unlikely it may seem at the time, the child does grow out of them.

Can they be treated?

If this is a repeated problem that your child suffers with, it is worth talking to your doctor to see whether you can be referred to the appropriate clinic. Drug treatment is generally considered to be ineffective and one of the current ways that experts are using to deal with the problem involves 'breaking' the child's sleep. In one study, parents were asked to look for signs that indicated a night terror was imminent. When a clear pattern was established, they were then asked to wake the child ten to fifteen minutes before the terror was due. After the child was kept awake for about five minutes, he was then allowed to go back to sleep. In the research into this method, within a week parents noticed that the terrors had stopped. In some cases they did return at a later stage, but by using the same method, the problem ceased. Apparently, the treatment works because it interrupts a fault in the deep sleep pattern which enables the child to return to a normal pattern of sleep.

your personalised directory of dream themes

As we've seen, one of the most fascinating aspects of dreaming is that there is absolutely no logic and no limits to it: you may suddenly find that you can fly, become a heroine for saving a whole village from death and destruction, or even find yourself taking tea with a long-dead relative.

However, while dreaming is obviously an individual business, what's interesting is that psychologists, as well as dream experts, have discovered that time and time again particular themes crop up when people are asked to recall their dreams. And that stands true for people who have different backgrounds and come from different cultures.

One example of this is that, apparently, most of us will dream of falling at some time, or being chased – often by persons unknown, regardless of what's gone on in our lives. And the same applies to dreams where we may find ourselves desperate to get away but unable to move, or even of having passionate sex with a relative stranger!

In some ways of course it's rather a blow to discover your dreams aren't quite that unique, but on the other hand it can be reassuring to hear that dreaming of something that brings you out in a cold sweat – be it caused by passion or fear – is not that uncommon. However, as we've seen, the meaning of a particular dream can only really be understood in the context of your reality: in other words, the way it's interpreted depends on what is going on in your life. So, before you start to work out what your dreams reveal, it's important to work from the basis that nothing is ever what it seems!

Below is a list of common dreams. We've listed them in order of theme because only when we think about a dream as a whole can we begin to understand its meaning. And although we all dream in images, it's only when we put those images together that we can attempt to make any sense out of them.

Before you start looking for meaning it can help to run through a quick mental check on any outside 'interference' that may have had some bearing on the dream. Remember, indigestion may influence your dream material as much as watching a violent film.

At first glance you may feel our list does not cover any of your dreams specifically. If that's the case, we suggest you read the interpretation for the theme that is most similar to yours and then try to gain a deeper understanding by following our key questions listed at the end of each section.

The themes

Being Chased

This is probably one of the most common dreams.

The Dream

The actual scene can be set in familiar surroundings (your local high street, for example) or even given a historical perspective by showing you being pursued by the 'enemy' as you race through wartorn Europe. However, the scene is a little like a sub-plot that's running through your life; what's really significant is the theme.

Such dreams are linked to anxiety and this is clearly indicated by the depth of emotion that such dreams cause. It's not uncommon for the dreamer to wake up with a start feeling totally disorientated as he attempts to make sense of the disturbing sequence of images that he has just experienced. Indeed some people have reported how it has taken several hours to shrug off the feelings of persecution that the dream has provoked.

The Meaning

You're running away from something, possibly trying to find a way of escaping from the problems in your life that are in danger of dominating every other aspect of your life. You may be frustrated, too, because you know you have obligations, possibly through no choice of your own, that have to be fulfilled. You feel pressurised but really don't know what to do about it, so it's hardly surprising that you dream of escaping from your present situation.

Stella spent a lot of her time running in her dreams. In one dream she found herself dreaming of being chased by a whole army squadron, in another by large clumps of indistinguishable individuals – none of whom meant anything to her. The dream wouldn't necessarily occur nightly but it would recur every six months or so. And each time she'd wake up in a cold sweat, trying to understand why.

In her waking life Stella's world couldn't have appeared more different. She was a successful marketing executive, happily married, with a 7-year-old child whom she clearly adored. She had reliable childcare and her managers at work thought highly of her and went to great lengths to assure her that she was earmarked for success.

So, what was the problem? In truth, Stella was constantly exhausted and felt continually overstretched by her dual commitments. Her managers were pleased with her performance but she knew that extra responsibility would mean more time would need to be devoted to – and spent at – work, which in turn would mean less time for her family. On top of this she knew that to get on to the next rung of the ladder she'd have to complete a number of courses – all of which were residential and often took place over the weekends. The issue of these courses was raised periodically and she knew that the day would come fairly soon when she would have to confront it. That said, she was avoiding it for as long as she possibly could.

As you can see, when Stella's dreams are put in context; it's not too difficult to understand her dream – or what it's trying to tell her. She knows that she is going to have to confront the problem but keeps trying to avoid it in the hope that it will go away – which of course it won't. If she did confront the problem headlong and was honest with her managers about her split loyalties she would be able to cope with the situation much better.

Stella needs to be the one to set the parameters of her job. Clearly she is well thought of and the company values her contribution, so if they are given the chance to understand her pressures they may be able to suggest alternative ways for her to receive the training she needs.

Alternatively, she may need to say that, at the present time, she actually doesn't want to advance any further – she's happy to stay where she is. It could well be that there are a number of options that could be explored but it's only when she begins to confront them that she will be able to organise her life in a way that she will be able to feel totally happy with. Her dream is telling her that she needs to face the pressures in her life if the situation is ever to be resolved.

If you're having this type of dream, it can also signify a type of hopelessness. You're in what you feel is a no-win situation and you simply don't know how to get out of it. In some cases you may need to look at who is doing the chasing. If it's someone in uniform you may be feeling pressurised by someone in a position of authority. It could be a teacher, or someone at work. Maybe it's a father-figure, which could imply that you are running away from family responsibilites. The character doing the pursuing could tell you something about the pressures you put on yourself – in other words the targets and standards you set yourself.

Making the dream work for you

To understand the totality of your dream, it may help to ask yourself some basic questions. For example:

- Have you taken on too much responsibility?

- Are you feeling under pressure?

- Do you feel that you're being taken advantage of?

- Are you generally feeling hassled by family, friends or work?

- Would you prefer to be doing less?

- Are you pushing yourself too far – or too hard?

Action

If the answer is 'yes' to the majority of the questions then it's time to try and disentangle yourself and, where possible, sort out your life in a way that makes you feel you are getting as much out of it as you're putting in. You may have to reassess your areas of priority and even scale down your ambitions for the time being.

If the problem is work, try to talk through your workload with a boss; if the problem is at home, try to work out a system whereby, whenever possible, responsibilities are shared with a partner, a neighbour or a friend. Try to identify how much pressure is coming from within, in other words yourself, and how much is down to external forces.

Look for short-cuts where possible and don't be embarrassed to ask for help where necessary. The key is to use your dream to solve problems – not simply repeat them.

Falling

Theories on this theme abound and such dreams are thought to be due to anything from muscle spasms to fear of failure.

The Dream
You could find yourself falling down an icy ravine, off a cliff, out of an aeroplane – even into a hole. The actual dream may also depict a whole sequence of events, some may be relatively uneventful, culminating in a fall.

The Meaning
Scientists believe that this falling sensation, which is so common amongst dreamers, may be due to actual physical changes that occur in our body as we sleep; it's part of the sensation of falling asleep. What seems to happen is that as we fall asleep it's not unusual for us to have an involuntary muscle spasm and the fall or sudden jerk we feel is simply the result of the muscles relaxing. This, as with 'external interference' such as alarm clocks and music, can become incorporated into the world of our dreams. The actual sensation can vary from a gentle feeling of falling to an almighty jerk which causes you to cling on to something for dear life! Whatever variety you have, and however often, muscle spasms are absolutely nothing to worry about.

As well as sudden spasms, other commentators have suggested

that dreams dominated by a falling theme could well be down to a very unmystical condition – indigestion, or possibly some sort of gastric grumbling, brought on by an overindulgent meal, too near bedtime.

Of course many dream analysts offer somewhat more sophisticated explanations. One belief is that falling signifies being out of control. Maybe all sorts of things are happening in your life that worry you, although none of them is related to your actions directly. In other words, external events are imposing limitations on what you can or cannot do.

Making the dream work for you

First you need to try to identify the areas of your life where there could be a link between a loss of control and your dream. Questions to ask yourself may be:

- Do you feel in total control of your life?

- Do you always make decisions that you feel happy with?

- When it comes to being in the driving seat, do you make the decisions?

- Are you happy with other people making decisions on your behalf?

- Is your life developing in the way that you want?

If you answer 'no' to most of the questions above, it may be time to listen to your dream.

Action

Try to divide your life up into compartments of, for example: family; work; colleagues; friends and leisure activities. Then go through each category, asking yourself just how much control you have. Obviously there are areas in all our lives where we have little or no control, but where you do have a say, it's important to assert yourself. So, if you don't like the way a relationship is going, something that's happening at work or even the division of labour that exists in your home (i.e. who does the dishes, the washing, and so on), then it may be time to take the bull by the horns.

It may also be worth considering whether your dream is warning you that it's time to take control of your life while you still can. Try to isolate the areas of your life where you can exert some control, rather than concentrating on the parts where you can't.

Flying, Floating

This is an extremely common dream that experts believe most of us will experience at some time or other.

The Dream
You may find yourself flying above your home town, just like Peter Pan, even being able to pick out friends and familiar places. Significantly, in most of these sorts of dreams the dreamer never rises very high – it's often more a case of floating over known territory, or simply being up above, looking down. Often the flyer has gained his newly elevated position in the same way a bird does – by simply flapping his wings and suddenly realising he's up in the air! Interestingly, for most people who have experienced this sort of dream, flying has always been effortless. Their bodies have floated around weightlessly and the whole experience is felt to be like an adventure.

The Meaning
Theories abound about this particular dream. One of the most common is that the flying signifies your ambition and how high and how easily you fly is defined in terms of the obstacles that

you encounter: the more you have to negotiate, the more likely it is that you're being over-ambitious. It could be said that if all your dream-time flapping results in various limbs being wrapped around telegraph poles, your present ambitions are, at this particular time, being thwarted, and it may be advisable to try and keep your feet on the ground!

Some interpreters also suggest that dreams of flying represent your ability to cope with events in your life: whatever happens you manage to rise above it – metaphorically at least. It also suggests that you have the ability to remain objective about what's going on – to stand on the outside rather than being weighed down by a complexity of feelings and emotions.

However, if you prefer a more esoteric theory, you might be interested in one current explanation that links flying to 'astral projection'. This is when 'your spirit is released', which means that it temporarily leaves your body, with the result that you are able to travel freely through time. It must be said that there is precious little research to support this view, but, as with many things spiritual, the theory certainly has its devotees.

Whichever explanation you feel is most relevant for you, it's worth mentioning that for most people, this dream inspires a positive feeling and dreamers have commented on being struck by an optimistic outlook when they wake up.

Making the dream work for you

Obviously to get to grips with the meaning of your dream you need to assess what it could be telling you about yourself.

So, try answering some of the questions below:

- Do you feel stretched at the moment?

- Have you set your heart on something – or somebody?

- Is there something that you are trying to distance yourself from?

- Have you a tendency to be over-ambitious?

Although in the language of dreams flying is deemed to be linked to ambitions, this doesn't have to be linked to work – in fact it's equally relevant if you've spent the best part of the last five years looking after children.

Action

What you need to concentrate on is your wider ambitions (for yourself, your family – even your bank balance) and decide just how realistic you are being. Is it possible that you're overstretching yourself? Are you being over-ambitious in your life and, just maybe, setting yourself up for a fall?

You also need to decide whether 'rising above' life is just another way of trying to avoid a situation that you fear may be unpleasant or confrontational. Often it can be far easier to float off into our own little world than confront something head-on. But what can be said about those people who positively enjoy the experience of dream-time flights of fancy? Well, our advice is to make the most of it. If, at the end of the day, you're happy circling up above, with no obstacles and no diversions, then probe no further – simply enjoy the trip!

Sex

The most widely known theory of sexually centred dreams is clearly Freud's. In fact it was Freud's opinion that all dreams – whatever their content – had some sexual basis. However, as we've seen in chapter 3, it's worth remembering that many of Freud's case histories were of people who had been referred to him for psychoanalytic treatment. The people he treated were clinical cases, and his many papers reflect their somewhat unusual personalities.

It is also worth mentioning that his theories have, to a certain extent, been superseded by more up-to-date interpretations that reflect our growing understanding of the subject. So, whilst his ideas are clearly the starting-point for our entry into the inner world of dreams, they by no means represent the limits of today's knowledge. Few people today would accept his view of many ordinary objects as sexual symbols: in other words, that anything even vaguely phallic, such as an umbrella, knife, train or tower, represents the penis, whilst anything surrounding it – boxes, tunnels, flowers and so on – represents female genitalia. He also considered that all dreams were about wish-fulfilment, although the dreamer probably wouldn't know it because of repressing the fact, either consciously or unconsciously.

To a large extent Freud's theories were a reflection of the times in which he lived. If we were to follow his belief that all women's dreams were almost always attributed to repressed, latent desires then we have to accept that this theory says much about him and the way women were perceived at the turn of the century. And it's worth remembering Freud also belonged to a society that took a repressive view of anything to do with sex.

Nowadays our understanding of psychology and of sexual and emotional development means that psychoanalysis has moved on from Freud's day – even though many theorists use Freud's basic concepts as a framework for analysis. However, much of his original work has been updated and most experts accept that sexual matters are not the only concerns that we have or, indeed, that manage to seep into the world of our dreams. Freud may have believed that through dream interpretation primal sexual desires and urges could be revealed as well as understood but today his approach – particularly his rigid sexual interpretation – is considered by most experts to be too narrow to always be constructive.

So, what does it mean when you dream about sex?

The Dream

One often-quoted example of dreams with this type of theme concerns a pregnant woman who, due to complications, was advised not to make love to her husband. Clearly this was a situation that neither one was happy with and she found herself regularly dreaming of wild orgies where she was the only female present. The men in her dream were all members of the cricket team to which her husband belonged but, interestingly, her husband didn't appear in the dream at all. She also noticed that in the morning she would wake up exhausted – having thoroughly enjoyed herself!

Other dreams of this nature can involve having sex with a stranger, someone you haven't seen for years, or maybe a person who is totally inappropriate, for example, your brother-in-law, the 'man in accounts' or some other anonymous person to whom you have never given a second thought. The actual sex can be tremendously enjoyable (as experienced by the lady and the cricket team!), fairly average or even downright unpleasant. And although you may find yourself playing an active part in the act, you could simultaneously see yourself standing on the sidelines, watching.

The Meaning

Theories on the subject are endless: anything from the blindingly obvious (dreaming of having sex means you're frustrated) to the relatively obscure. For some the dream is blatantly one of wish-fulfilment. This can be seen in the case of people who increasingly dream of sex with their partner while in reality their sex life is considerably diminished – due to lack of time, energy or even lack of attraction. Once the connection is made between 'the more you dream, the less you do', then the solution to the problem is easily identified – even if it's not quite so easy to execute!

Clearly the way you feel about the act has some bearing on what the dream could mean to you. The woman who enjoyed carnal knowledge with her husband's cricket team was clearly frustrated and, knowing that she wasn't able to have sex with her husband, unconsciously tried to gain satisfaction elsewhere.

One analyst suggests that if you enjoyed the experience then it's an omen of happiness – although that presumably did not take any account of the guilt the woman may have felt afterwards. Likewise some theorists believe that if you don't enjoy the sex then you are simply repressing an emotional problem, perhaps because you are stuck in a stale relationship. However, once again dreams of this kind must be put into context. If, say, you have had a strict religious upbringing, which has led you to associate sex very strongly with guilt, the dream may reflect an inner conflict more than any real repression.

Dreams of having sex with an 'inappropriate' or long-forgotten person do not automatically imply that you harbour secret desires: the explanation is likely to be much more mundane. If you were to trace back to the last time you had any contact with that person (either firsthand or somebody saying something that reminded you of them or events that you had shared) the chances are that some sort of 'connection' was made in the twenty-four hours preceding your dream. As we've seen in chapter 5, the content of our dreams is often influenced by events that have recently taken place – however insignificant they may have seemed at the time. So having sex with 'someone from accounts' could be due to nothing more significant than that you happened to see him at the coffee machine that morning and, somehow, your brain had registered that fact.

Other common dreams along this theme concern lovers or beds, where the sexual act is never consummated. Maybe the person disappears, or is transformed into someone, or something, else. In extreme cases, people have relayed tales of beds catching fire. These sorts of dreams can indicate one of two things. First, that you are dissatisfied (not necessarily sexually) with a relationship; you may feel that it's stagnated or suspect that you may not be compatible. Maybe you suspect you're the only one who's trying to make things work. The other explanation is related more to anxiety. It could be, for instance, that you have had a string of relationships that have been unsuccessful, for whatever reasons, and you are worried that your present relationship will go the same way. If in the dream you are clearly dominating events this may mean that there could be a power struggle going on in the relationship, or that you feel dominated in life generally by your partner and the dream is a way of trying to reverse this pattern.

Making the dream work for you

Try to analyse your existing relationships. Ask yourself:

- Am I stuck in a rut?

- Do I feel the relationship is unbalanced?

- Am I keeping the relationship going for the wrong reasons?

- Could the relationship be improved?

- Is sex important to me?

- Do I feel negative about sex?

If you've answered 'yes' to most of the questions, it could be time to think about exactly what you want from a relationship – whether it's a present one or one in the future.

Action

On a basic level, if you are actually dissatisfied with your sex life you need to bring the problem out into the open. Try discussing it with your partner and see whether he/she shares any of your concerns. The same rule applies for your relationship generally. If you feel that there is an unequal division of power between the two of you it is important to try to resolve the difficulties before you both become so entrenched in your roles that it would be difficult for either of you to give way.

On a simpler level, dreams of a sexual nature could simply be down to the fact that you'd like sex to play a larger part in your life but never quite manage it. Maybe you have young children and are still trying to cope with the interruptions of broken nights and early mornings, or possibly you and/or your partner have a lifestyle that means the amount of time you have for each other is minimal. If that's the case then, somehow, you both need to arrange your lives so that you can have more time for each other. Either get a babysitter, cancel arrangements or try to leave work on time – at least occasionally.

The only other point worth making where dreams such as this are concerned is that if you feel your relationship could do with some improvement (even if the only way you could really improve it is by ending it), then it certainly won't hurt to let your dream act as a trigger. However, if both you and your partner are perfectly happy with your relationship then the best way to handle these dreams is just to lie back and enjoy them!

Everyone's watching you

For many of us this type of dream can leave an unnerving feeling, long after we've woken up. And, although the dream scene may change, the theme is surprisingly common. There is also little logic attached to such events.

The Dream
There really are literally hundreds of variations on this theme. You could find yourself walking in the middle of a busy shopping precinct, only to realise suddenly – to your utter horror –

that you've forgotten to put any pants on. And to make matters worse, everyone can see. Or maybe you dream of happily sitting on the toilet, secure in a private world, when suddenly the door flies open. Everyone is staring at you and all you can do is sit, exposed, rather pathetically trying to cover up your 'private parts'. On a slightly different tack, you may dream of arriving at a smart, sophisticated dinner party. The other guests are wearing evening dress – dinner jackets, flowing gowns, that sort of thing – while you turn up in grubby shorts and a faded old tee-shirt. And everybody is staring at you . . .

The Meaning
This is really all about feeling exposed and nurturing a sense of shame. The dream itself is not so much about what you're wearing – or not wearing for that matter – but more about how you're feeling about your attire. One expert believes that for many of us a sense of embarrassment and shame is linked with being naked and our attitudes to nudity, as well as our attitudes towards dressing 'appropriately' for the occasion. The embarrassment, and to a certain extent, humiliation, that we feel when we discover that our appearance is inappropriate is something that most of us dread. Hence, activities that we may prefer to keep to ourselves can be revealed in our dreams.

Some experts feel that such dreams can signify your fear of someone discovering 'the real you'. Maybe you don't feel secure enough, either at work or over a relationship with a friend or someone in your family, so you are trying to let them see only the best part of you, scared that if you revealed all, it might put them off. Or maybe you simply feel guilty over something, however minor, and you're worried that someone may find out. It could also be that you're anxious about being picked out in a crowd and you feel happier being a foot soldier than a general, although someone has made you think that you may have to make a stand, or take a leading role over something.

Making the dream work for you

If you are having dreams which are leaving you feeling exposed and vulnerable, ask yourself the following questions:

- Have you anything to hide?

- Are you being completely honest with the people you know – as well as yourself?

- Are you being put in the position of being expected to do something that you'd rather not do?

- Have you taken on too much – either at home or at work?

- Do you have a tendency to get things out of perspective?

- Do you find that you're not always as prepared for events as you could be?

If you have answered 'yes' to most of the questions above, then it may be an opportunity to review some of the things that are happening in your life.

Action

If you are worried that someone may 'find something out' about the real you, ask yourself whether you are worrying unnecessarily. Does it really matter whether they discover you get impatient, lose your temper, or sometimes feel tired? Is it possible that you're making unrealistic demands of yourself?

If you feel that someone is expecting more than you can currently give, then it's important to assert yourself and be honest. That way you get to stay in control of the situation rather than the other way round – which is what would happen if any weakness that you feel you have is uncovered. Be honest about what you can and can't do. In the long term you can't help but benefit.

And if you are trying to hide something? Whatever it is, if you're having dreams about it then it is clearly preying on your mind which means the chances are that it isn't doing you any good. So try to off-load your secret, perhaps by sharing it with one other person you trust, and be more confident about the decisions you make. If you made the decision to do something a particular way, you obviously had your reasons. So, be confident in yourself – the more confident you are, the less you will worry about some unsatisfactory aspect of yourself being exposed.

Death

Often this can be one of the most disturbing themes – particularly if you dream of the death of someone close to you. However, as with other dreams, they are rarely what they seem.

The Dream

You're sitting down, maybe at your home or the home of a close relative, having a perfectly sensible conversation. You're discussing what you're doing, where you've been, your worries – a normal sort of conversation that you may have with anyone that you're close to. The only difference here is that the person you're talking to passed away years ago . . .

Another variation of this common theme is when you dream that someone close to you is dying, or maybe has just died, and you find yourself completely distraught and trying to deal with the event. Alternatively, you may dream about your own death: perhaps it has already taken place, or you may still be in the throes of dying.

The Meaning

Dreams about death can be viewed on either a symbolic or practical level. The one that is most appropriate will depend on what is going on in your life and how it is affecting you personally.

Symbolically, death represents not so much an ending as a new beginning. Commentators believe that to dream of your own death simply means that you are preparing to start something new in your life, maybe embarking on a new adventure, a new job or a new relationship. The symbolic association is about how part of you is being born again and is preparing for new beginnings. Some dream experts believe that to dream of a death frequently could actually mean that you will hear news of a real birth, while others emphasise that dreams of death herald new beginnings for the dreamer in a wider context.

However, these types of dreams could well have a more fundamental role to play for the dreamer. Dreaming of the death of someone close to you can be an almost subconscious way of preparing ourselves for such events that, in certain cases, have an inevitability about them that can't be ignored. So, it's possible that our dreams act as a sort of preparation by allowing us to come to terms with a bereavement which in turn will mean that hopefully, when the dream becomes reality, the trauma may be at least a little less distressing.

If your dreams concern relatives who have recently passed away, then you may find that the dream is helping you to come to terms with your grief – particularly if the dream depicts you and the relative in question having conversations about things that you would always would have liked to have discussed but, somehow, never quite got around to. It also allows you to feel that, in some ways, although that person has died, it doesn't necessarily mean that they have disappeared from your life.

But what of dreams of people who have long since left us? For some people what may be relevant is the role that that person played in your life. So, you may find, for no reason at all, that you are dreaming of your grandmother who died when you were still a child. Your memory of her may still be intrinsically linked with the comfort and love that you, unquestionably, always received from her. In your mind, that association still remains and maybe you find yourself dreaming of her when you're in particular need of love – or support. And the same would be true if you were to dream of a parent on whom you always relied for guidance. If you find that you're at a time in your life when you need to make a decision – but can't decide which way to go – it is understandable that, subconsciously, you 'call up' the people that you know you can most rely upon to rally round you. And the chances are that just dreaming about them can offer comfort, regardless of any real or imagined conversations.

Making the dream work for you

To put the dream in perspective, try asking yourself some basic questions. For example:

- Is your life taking an unexpected turn?

- Are you starting a new job?

- Are you beginning a new relationship?

- Do you worry about the health of a relative or friend?

- Do you feel you could do with some extra support?

- Could you do with sharing your dilemmas and problems?

If you answered 'yes' to the majority of these questions, then you may benefit from reading our action plan.

Action
If you are feeling the lack of someone who can offer you guidance or comfort then maybe it's time to share some of your feelings with people around you. Given the chance,

most people are keen to offer support when they can. Although it can often feel like new friends can never replace the old, people that we meet in our adult lives will invariably reflect our adult selves more than the people whom we have known since we were children.

If you find that you are going through periods of being preoccupied with the longevity of someone you're close to, it's important to put such thoughts in context. Are they irrational? Have you cause to worry? Sometimes such fears can be triggered by events that have happened to people you know. Maybe a friend has recently lost a parent, or a partner, which inevitably concentrates your mind on the people *you* know.

Such concerns are perfectly natural and, what's more, we all have them from time to time. That said, if possible it is important not to dwell on such thoughts as they can end up working against you by causing depression and feelings of self-pity. If, however, you can actually link your dreams to new beginnings in your life then simply recognise them for what they are – and get on with your new beginning, whatever it may be.

Being Late

The Dream

As with many themed dreams, this particular one can manifest itself in many ways although the example given here is one that Alison experiences regularly, every few weeks.

I'm always going somewhere, although I'm never really sure where it is I'm going. The journey demands an awful lot of effort but I never seem to be actually getting anywhere – it's a little like walking through treacle. I also never seem to never pick up any of my connections fast enough. All that I know is that a bus, a train, a boat – it could be anything – is always on its way and I absolutely have to catch it . . . but I never actually manage to. When I finally wake up I'm quite emotionally exhausted by the effort of it all.

Other people who have similar dreams report getting to the station in time to see the train pulling away; arriving at the airport – only to remember that they were getting the boat – or being on a bus that encounters problem after problem, all resulting in them getting later and later to wherever they're going.

The Meaning

As with all dreams, the meaning will vary depending on particular circumstances in the life of the person concerned. Alison, for example, never feels totally in control of her life as her job as a freelance hairdresser involves her rushing around all over the place, trying to please a variety of clients all at the same time – which frequently proves impossible because she takes on too much work. As a self-employed person, she is reluctant to say no to would-be customers, even when she's busy, in case the phone stops ringing and her income dries up. What's more, she lives in a busy city, so she can often spend a fair part of her day either stuck in traffic or on a train. So, being on time is a very real concern to her and her dreams clearly reflect this pressure.

For other people who have similar chaotic experiences during their REM sleep, the underlying message is the same: in the dream, all their daily stress is being amalgamated into one sizeable chunk which should make it crystal clear what problems they are constantly creating for themselves. If you're stressed enough about your timetable to be able to dream about it, you may just have to accept that your daily activities would benefit from some serious efforts at rationalisation.

Some dream analysts also believe that this type of dream is representative of ambition as well as self-esteem: ambition because everything you do is seen in terms of goals (must catch the plane, can't miss the train); and self-esteem because yours is so low that you define everything in terms of what you can achieve. You set yourself goals and assess your success in terms of what you can do – for some reason you do not have enough confidence in yourself to see that achieving is not necessarily measured in terms of goals. Real achievement is much more subtle than that; real achievement is to do with feeling good about yourself – regardless of whether you get the 7.10 or the 7.20.

Making the dream work for you

If this is a dream you know only too well, try asking yourself some of the following questions:

- Do you ever worry about being late?

- Are you ever late?

- Do you think you're overstretched?

- Are you attracted by a change of lifestyle?

- Do you think you could do with more time for yourself?

- Do you ever feel you push yourself too hard?

If you have said 'yes' to most of the above questions, now is the time to act!

Action
Admittedly, trying to balance all the elements in our lives can be a delicate business but with careful planning and realistic organisation it is possible. First, you need to take a candid look at your life and ask whether you are forcing

yourself to do too much in too short a time. By trying to please everybody you may well find that the person who is truly suffering is yourself.

Try to balance your life more. Work out what can reasonably be achieved in any one given day and don't take on anything else. As long as you don't leave things too long, people will wait. And anyway, given the choice, almost everybody would rather have a good job done a day or so late than a bad job that may have been completed on time but which, because it has been done in too much of a rush, has to be done again or reworked.

Be fair to yourself. And learn to say no. If someone is pushing you too hard you need to stand up for yourself. If you don't, then the chances are nobody else will.

Fear of Failing

The Dream
Sian's dream is fairly typical of this type of theme.

I almost always dream exactly the same scene: I'm standing outside an exam room but it's not any exam room – it's where I took my finals. There's a group of us and it's the same people that I took my exams with. We're all standing there discussing what might come up but I'm terrified because I know I haven't revised properly so there's no way I'm going to be able to answer any questions. It's ghastly and what makes it worse is that I know it's too late to do anything about it . . . I'm going to fail.

Although in this dream no test is actually taken, many people report dreams where they're sitting an exam but don't know any of the answers. Others have told of dreams where they find themselves in a classroom and are filled with anxiety. The same theme, albeit set in a different scene, is when the dreamer sees herself opening the door to dinner guests in a state of great agitation because although they were clearly expected, she hasn't prepared a single thing for the occasion.

The Meaning

In Sian's case, it's worth mentioning that she had no problem passing her exams and now, at 34, she is a successful designer. But her life is filled with a multitude of deadlines. Not surprisingly, her dreams reflect this as a series of exams – which, in a sense, is what they are. Interestingly, Sian has these dreams when she is feeling more stressed than normal about work. Clearly she worries that she's not 'going to make it' and that she's going to let people down because she's overstretched. And, subconsciously, she could also be worried that she's being overambitious.

Similiar dreams tell the same tale, whether the person sees themselves cooking dinner for guests or suddenly catapulted into a classroom of children where everyone knows what they're supposed to be doing, everyone except the dreamer.

This type of dream is clearly showing that the dreamer is anxious about fulfilling her obligations. She feels overstretched and is worried she'll fail. She's also likely to be a perfectionist and however much she has prepared for an impending job, test or dinner party, she will never accept that she's done enough

Making the dream work for you

If this dream is a 'one-off' for you then your best bet is to accept it as a subconscious attempt to cope with the the specific pressures that you are currently under. And be warned that it's not advisable for anyone to put themselves under sustained pressure – either physically, mentally or emotionally. However, if this is a recurring dream, try asking yourself the following questions:

- Have you taken on too much recently?

- Do you feel things are getting on top of you?

- Is it possible that you're setting yourself unrealistic goals?

- Could you do with slowing you life down a little?

- Are you anxious to do everything not just well but perfectly?

If you have said 'yes' to the majority of the above questions, it may be time to reassess your present situation.

Action

Think about whether you are setting yourself unrealistic targets. Is there any way you can share some of your responsibilities? Does everything really have to be done 'yesterday'? Is it possible to renegotiate times of delivery, or deadlines? You also need to explore whether you are setting yourself standards that are almost impossible to achieve. Is it possible to do all the work you've taken on? Do you have to make a formal five-course meal for friends when a simple supper might do? You may also have to accept that there are occasions when you have to compromise and, at times, even learn the art of saying no!

You should also ask yourself whether you might be taking on burdens that do not rightly belong on your shoulders. For example, if a job you are involved in goes wrong, is it really because you didn't do your part? It's all too easy to get into the habit of blaming yourself for everything when in reality it was someone else who let the side down by not fulfilling their end of the bargain.

Royalty

Such dreams are more common than you might think. However, what's often particularly significant about them is that they are almost always totally illogical!

The Dream

Generally these dreams take place in the comfort of your home and can involve anything from taking tea with the Queen to chatting on the phone to Prince Charles. Or you might even find yourself down at the local gym – sharing an exercise class with Princess Diana! Often the dreams are quite vivid and so when you wake up you can still 'see' Her Majesty perched on the end of your sofa, drinking tea out of your best china as you offer her some of your infamous home-made fruit cake. The dream itself is often an uncomfortable mix of the ordinary (your front room) with the extraordinary (the Queen chatting happily to you, agreeing that yes, children can be a worry, can't they . . .).

The Meaning

You may not be too surprised to hear that such dreams never have a literal meaning and are always symbolic! So, if you think this type of theme is a premonition of an impending royal relationship, you are likely to be somewhat disappointed!

Although some commentators see the Queen as a sort of Mother Nature figure, dispensing wisdom to all, many experts believe the royal family symbolises anyone in your life who plays a dominant role. So, for some it may be their father, or a father-like figure, for others it may be the Chief Executive of their company or their branch manager – anyone in fact who has some influence over your life, whether short-term or long-term.

The 'visit' could reflect your concern about the level of interference there is in your life: it may be from family, friends or someone at work. Maybe you feel that so many people are advising you over what you should be doing that they're not giving you a chance to think about what you want to do.

After having this sort of dream, you need to give some thought to how you actually feel during the dream. Were you terrified? Maybe you were worried that you weren't 'good enough' to be entertaining Royals. Or did you resent that, the visitor having suddenly appeared, you were forced to put everything you were doing on hold until the visit was over? The way you felt could be an indication of how you're feeling about some of the people who have a role to play in influencing what you do.

Making the dream work for you

If you think there may be some connection between your present situation and your dream, see if any of the questions below are relevant to you.

- Is there somebody who you feel is having an adverse effect on your life?

- Do you feel most of what you do is determined by other people?

- Do you tend to avoid confrontation?

- Are you worried about recent problems in a relationship?

- Would you like to feel you had more influence over your life?

If you have answered 'yes' to any of the questions above, it may be worth putting some of your relationships under the spotlight.

Action

If you suspect that you're avoiding a confrontation with someone then it may be time to face them. Confrontations don't always have to be negative. If you do feel that you're not in total control of your life try to take charge. Isolate the areas where you could have control if maybe you were a little more honest about how you felt and what you wanted to do.

If you do feel that a parent or someone who is in a position of authority in your life seems to be 'taking over' it's important to deal with the problem before it gets out of hand. However, before you dispense with all father-like figures, be sure that what you really want isn't some good old-fashioned advice. Your dream may subconsciously be trying to tell you that really what you need in your life is guidance, and the best person to turn to could be someone older, and, certainly in your opinion, wiser. And they don't have to be wearing a crown to have something to say that's worth listening to!

Water

Although this is one of the top theme dreams, it can appear in any one of a number of forms.

The Dream

You're standing on the deck of a boat, or ship, staring out into the distance. All you can see is sea. Yet you don't necessarily feel concerned about this – if anything the scene has a calming effect; you're serene and thoughtful although not necessarily conscious of anything or anybody.

Or you may see yourself swimming – irrespective of whether you can actually do this in your waking life – happily enjoying the stillness of the water.

Alternatively you could be surrounded by water, but not out of choice. Maybe you're caught up in a scene from a flood or you see yourself struggling with someone while you're both standing in the sea, or a stream.

The Meaning

Obviously your relationship to the water is significant. Dreams of water generally reflect life changes. People who have reached a specific stage in their life (marriage, children, grandchildren) report dreams of this nature and some experts link these water themes with the ending of one phase of your life and the beginning of another. So, maybe you're beginning a new relationship, or a new job? Or have you finally decided to put something from the past behind you and make a fresh start?

If you find the water threatening in the dream and there is something that you're worried about in your waking life, it is easy to interpret your dream as a reflection of what is really going on in your world. However, a more Freudian-based belief is that dreams of water indicate a latent desire to return to the security and protection of the womb. An updated version of this suggests that the dreamer is feeling insecure about something and that insecurity is invading the night world as well as the daytime one.

Some commentators believe that the difficulties that the water presents to you in the dream can also have some bearing on what it means. So, for example, if you're trying to cross a river and it's a task easily done then you can achieve your immediate goals with little problem. If, however, the crossing is beset with problems (and anything from choppy water to crocodiles can constitute a problem) then you may have to consider whether, for the moment, you're setting your sights too high.

Equally, if the water is calm and flowing gently, some dream analysts would say this indicates that your life is about to enter a period of inner contentment.

Making the dream work for you

If water does seem to be a dominant theme in your dreams, then it may be worth considering the following questions:

- Are you about to enter a new phase of your life?

- Has something significant recently happened?

- Has a relationship, or job, recently come to an end?

- Do you feel vulnerable?

- Do you long for more security in your life?

- Are you trying to tackle some task which could be too much for you?

If you've said 'yes' to most of the questions above, it could be worth taking stock of exactly where you're going in life.

Action

If you are entering a new phase in your life or starting out on something new, don't rush at things. Just enjoy what you're doing – and who you're doing it with – for the moment without trying to impose deeper meanings on events when it may not be appropriate. Let things happen and enjoy them for what they are. If, on the other hand, you are feeling vulnerable and insecure it may be time to explore exactly why. Are you trying to make things in your life happen faster than they can? Are you reading more into a relationship than you should? If you can identify the source of your insecurity, you may be able to do something about it – talk about problems in a relationship, or simply confide your worries to a sympathetic friend. Getting someone else's point of view on your concerns may help to put them into perspective.

If, however, events or people in your life are conspiring to make you feel isolated then it may be an idea to stop sticking your neck out. Let someone else be at the forefront of events and take the lead for a bit. At the end of the day you need to feel confident about what you're doing in life, whether it concerns relationships or work. If you don't feel right about what you're doing, then no amount of thrusting out into the limelight is going to change that. Try doing right by yourself and the chances are that you'll find everything else will then simply fall into place.

Food

As with dreams of water, the significance of these types of dreams depends on your relationship to the food that you're dreaming about – so the meaning can vary.

The Dream

You're at a banquet and everyone is having a wonderful time. The food is plentiful and the place is overflowing with exotic fruits and tantalising dishes. The problem is that you don't feel you can join in. You just don't feel right being there, almost as if you've been invited to join in a game but nobody has bothered to tell you the rules.

And although all the food is wonderfully tempting, it doesn't look anything like the food you're used to eating so you're doing your utmost to avoid it – just because you're not quite sure what to do with it. Another variation on this theme might be that although you know that you're heartily tucking in, in reality you're not actually getting any enjoyment from what you're apparently eating.

The Meaning

Abstaining from eating in a dream can mean several things. One interpretation is that you're feeling out of your depth. The food represents something in your life that you just can't cope with. Hence the fact that you opt for avoiding the food rather than just eating, for fear of making a fool of yourself. And the sense that you're not joining in can also emphasise your fear of being an outsider – someone who is always standing on the sidelines rather than being in the midst of the activity.

Not too surprisingly, self-indulgence with food can be seen as an indication of greed, although many present-day commentators believe that there are other factors involved. It could indicate that people regard you as someone who throws yourself into all that's going on around you, whereas in truth, you know that you're holding back. If your cautiousness is in the area of relationships, and especially in emotional commitment, this may be because you've been hurt and are trying to protect yourself. So, if you dream of satisfying your primal urge of hunger but without receiving any of the pleasure associated with eating, this may reflect a tendency to hold back in relationships, and to avoid 'letting go'.

Also, if we see food as symbolic and representing the emotional support in our lives, then it's possible to consider overindulgence as relating to emotional immaturity or reflecting an inability to be emotionally satisfied with your relationships. Maybe you're in the throes of a dying relationship but don't know how to extricate yourself; or maybe you're in a dead-end job and, although you hate it, you have tried to reconcile yourself to that fact that you can't get anything better.

It's also worth bearing in mind the role the food plays in your life. If you work with food, or spend much of your time cooking and preparing it, the dream may have a different meaning than for someone whose contact with food is generally only when they sit down to eat it. So, dreams to do with something that takes up much of your waking life may indicate that you simply have too much to do, you're unprepared – or you're in desperate need of a break.

Making the dream work for you

If your dreams of food are pleasurable and leave you with a feeling of satisfaction, there is obviously little point in dwelling on them too much. However, if the dreams leave you with an uneasy feeling, it might be as well to ask yourself the following questions:

• Are you feeling isolated?

• Do you feel friends leave you out of activities?

• Are you emotionally frustrated?

• Do you find it hard to trust people?

• Do you wish you had more confidence?

• Would you like to get more involved in life – but aren't quite sure how to?

• Do you ever feel out of your depth?

If you answered 'yes' to the majority of questions, it may be worth seeing how you can make the dream work for you.

Action

If you feel out of your depth socially then it means you're mixing with the wrong people. And if you feel the same way mentally, it could indicate frustration due to the fact that you suspect your skills and talents are going largely unrecognised.

Socially, it may help to widen your circle of friends or even explore new friendships by following up any special interests that you may have. Try to spend more time with people with whom you feel you genuinely have something in common or those who like you. There's little point in throwing yourself into a frantic social round which gives you little or no actual pleasure. If work is getting you down then you need to start thinking about your next move. There may not be a job instantly available, but if you're mentally geared up for a move, when a suitable job comes up, at least you will feel motivated to apply for it.

Dealing with emotional dissatisfactions can be more difficult but the most crucial factor is to be honest with yourself. Try to work out why you feel as you do and explore possible solutions, If it involves someone else, talk to them about your feelings. If you feel dissatisfied in a relationship, the chances are the other person does too. Trying to find a solution to the problem could be in both your interests.

When you can't move

A fairly classic anxiety dream is when you are unable to move and this has a specific meaning.

The Dream
You're in a lift, often alone, and suddenly it stops. You press the buttons and nothing happens. You ring the alarm bell – and nothing happens. You shout and no one hears you. But worse than that, you're unable to hear anything, except possibly the beating of your heart. Essentially you're alone and there's no one who can help you.

Another common variation on this theme is where you feel threatened. You may be at home, at work, or in a strange place that you can't recognise. Suddenly, though, you are aware of the presence of a stranger. You know they're coming after you – or possibly even after your loved ones – but there's nothing that you can do about it. You find yourself unable to move, or call out. It's as if you're stuck or frozen or rooted to the spot.

The Meaning
Some experts believe that such dreams are related to a reluctance

to make changes in your life – changes that could be physical as well as emotional. Possibly you're scared of change, believing intrinsically in the old adage, 'Better the devil you know'. Yet your dream is saying that, at some level, you're not content with the situation as it is, however alarming the prospect of changing it might initially seem to you.

It may also show that you are feeling frustrated about something in your life – maybe there's something going on over which you feel you have little control. So, it could be that you feel stuck in a cleft stick – rather than suspended in a broken-down lift. Things are happening to you, or to your family, but you feel there is little you can do about it. You can't think of anyone you can turn to for help, yet it seems you are powerless to act on your own.

These dreams are often experienced by people who are going through a particularly stressful period – maybe your employment is threatened or, even worse, non-existent. Maybe a sudden unexpected call on your finances has left you in a state of financial insecurity. Or it could even be that the ending of a relationship has been notably acrimonious – which has all sorts of knock-on effects for your family as well as yourself.

On a more scientific level, some experts believe this feeling of paralysis can be explained in terms of the physical sensations that affect our body when we sleep. During REM sleep, as we've seen in chapter 2, our muscles are in a flaccid state; in other words, we literally cannot move. Apart from flicking our eyeballs around behind closed lids, we have temporarily lost the ability to move arms, legs or any other part of our bodies; only those muscles which aren't under voluntary control, such as the heart and those controlling breathing, are still working. At some level, even if not consciously, we are aware of this unpleasant state of affairs, and scientists believe that these types of dreams are a subconscious response to our inability to move. The reason we don't all have these sorts of dreams the whole time is thought to be because they only occur when we try to move during our REM sleep.

Making the dream work for you

Worry about protecting ourselves and our families is all too common in the seemingly dangerous and often violent world in which we live. What's more, newspaper coverage of suffering and aggression can bring those concerns to the forefront of our mind. And of course the most disturbing element of such events is that we are rendered powerless. Horrendous acts of evil can, potentially, happen to someone we know and love and yet we have no control over them. These fears can clearly prey on our minds, never more so than when a particularly gruesome case has come to light – a case where more often than not we are given a blow-by-blow account of what has happened. No wonder then that this becomes the stuff of our dreams and the focus of our anxiety.

So, if you do find that these thoughts and fears seem to be a recurring theme in your dreams, it may be worth monitoring just how much of the day's news is seeping into your subconscious. If there is a strong link between what's happening in the external world and your dream world then you need not look any further for meaning. Often such dreams need no interpretation. However, if there is no such link, it may be worth asking yourself the following questions:

- Do you feel you have little control in your life?

- Do you hate change?

- Would you like to have more control?

- Are you scared of making the wrong decisions?

- Do you feel you have too much responsibility?

If you've said 'yes' to the majority of these questions, you may feel the need to take action.

Action

If you suspect your problem is that you have an innate fear of change, then a good starting-point is to acknowledge that change can be positive. It can herald new beginnings and breathe new life into a situation. So, to a certain extent, negativity can be as much about your perception of events as about the events themselves. Try seeing change as an adventure or an exciting opportunity rather than as a huge risk. Everything we do is an experience that we can ultimately learn from and recognising that is half-way to accepting that change is an important part of life, as well as of your own personal development.

If you feel that things are happening around you with little concern being paid to you, then it's up to you to try to reverse the trend. Make your thoughts known and, where possible, try to have an impact on some of the events that are important in your life. Admittedly it is often difficult, if not impossible, to influence major changes in the wider world, but making a contribution in a relatively minor way can still be constructive and helpful. For example, you could start out by letting your views contribute to a local environmental group, or working party at the place where you work, or campaigning for a cause that seems important to you. And, more importantly, at least it will show you that, even in a small way, we all have the power to make a difference.

Foreseeing the Future

According to some studies, hundreds of people dream of some future event every night. In some cases, of course, the dream may be linked to a foregone conclusion: for example, a dream that depicts you packing up crockery when a house move is imminent. However, not all such experiences can be so easily explained and dreams of the future have occupied the minds of commentators since the beginnings of recorded history, as we've seen in chapter 4. Thousands of years before Christ the Egyptians wrote of revelations that appeared in their dreams, as did the Ancient Greeks and the authors of the Bible. Both the Old and New Testaments, as well as folklore and mythology, are full of such tales. Somewhat more recently experts have attempted to understand this phenomenon, usually known as 'precognitive dreaming'.

The Dreams

Jung, in particular, believed that dreams could foretell the future and he wrote of one particularly chilling experience when he dreamt of winds sweeping through Europe, freezing the land to ice. He dreamt of a deserted area where vegetation had been killed by frost and there was a complete absence of human life. The dream occurred in June 1914 – just two months before the First World War was declared.

Of course it is possible to explain Jung's dream, in as much as it reflected the times in which he was living. The newspapers would have been full of events in Europe and the likelihood is that just about everyone would have been talking about what was going on and speculating on the possible outcome. So, the dream didn't actually come from 'nowhere' – it is more likely to have been a result of educated thoughts moulded together that ultimately manifested themselves as a classic anxiety dream.

One example of a possible precognitive dream that is not quite so easily explained is the well-documented experience of John Williams, in 1933. As a Quaker, Williams was a lifelong opponent of betting as well as drinking and smoking. It happened on Derby Day, when he dreamt he was listening to a radio commentary of the race and heard the commentator say the names of the winners – two of which he managed to remember.

For Williams it was a particularly strange dream to have as he took absolutely no interest in racing and certainly never read about it. But, to his utter amazement the two remembered names turned out to be the winner and runner-up of the race! The actual incident was investigated by a credible expert of that time and the conclusion was that Mr Williams' dream could only be explained in terms of precognition.

Tales abound of people recalling dreams where some significant event has been foreseen. One woman in 1981 told how she dreamt of President Sadat's assassination and the shooting of the then President Reagan, while author Graham Greene has written of his momentous dream when he was a young child of a horrendous shipwreck. He then discovered that that very same night the Titanic had sunk.

Foreseeing tragic events in our dreams is not necessarily a unique experience. In 1966 a 10-year-old girl was so disturbed by her dream which showed something black covering her school that she initially refused to attend that day. Having been calmed down by her mother she eventually did go. But tragically it was the day when disaster hit the school in Aberfan, leaving it, with many pupils, buried under a black heap of coal slag, which had collapsed, burying the whole school.

On a more personal scale, although no less traumatic for the dreamer, many people have stories which tell of dreams where relatives have died – only to hear within days that the relative concerned had passed away. Susan, now 30, remembers dreaming vividly many years ago of standing in a graveyard surrounded by lots of people – none of whom she recognised, while someone was being buried. In the background was a church, distinctive because of its pointed roof and ornate spire. Two years later her father died unexpectedly. She went to the funeral which was held at a church she had never been to before and as she was standing by the graveside she was suddenly overcome by a powerful sense of *déjà vu*. Then as she looked up, she caught sight of the church – which was exactly the same as the one in her dream, and situated in exactly the same place as she'd seen from her dream graveside.

The Meaning

According to some scientists, we will dream a dream of the future twice in our lives. Why this is, can be difficult to answer conclusively. After many years of studying the subject, clinical psychologist David Ryback believes that there is some primitive mechanism at work warning us of impending disasters. To support this theory he tells of a woman who dreamt of a lorry crashing into her car. Soon after, in her waking world, when she found herself approaching the traffic lights that appeared in her dream just before the crash, she was able to take evasive action.

Ryback also relays the story, as do other commentators, of people dreaming that they are being operated on or diagnosed as having a fatal illness. The dream concerns them so much that they eventually see their doctor, only to discover that they are suffering from a serious condition, although the timing of their visit has often ensured swift diagnosis which has resulted in effective treatment that has managed to control the condition and even save their lives.

Clearly there are many stories which appear to support this theory, although even experts like Ryback acknowledge that, while they are convinced that certain dreams can tell the future, they are still unsure how. Women are supposed to experience more dreams of the future than men, although this may be due to the fact that women tend to be more open about what's happening in their lives than men and, due to our culture, are more at ease discussing a relatively inexact subject like dreams.

There have been a number of attempts to assess just how reliable these types of dreams are. After the Aberfan disaster, so many people reported having dreams that foretold the tragedy that a Premonitions Bureau was set up so that all the information concerning warning dreams could be monitored. Interestingly, although the dreams of those who lived near the scene of the tragedy (and who were therefore aware of the potential threat of the tip) could simply have been reflecting natural anxiety, it is hard to dismiss the fact that many other people from other parts of the country claimed to have had relevant precognitive dreams. Some of the dreamers had probably never even heard the name of Aberfan before the disaster – or their dream – struck.

Although the Premonitions Bureau remained in existence for many years, the experts concerned claimed there was very little scientific evidence for the existence of precognitive dreams. That said, it is notoriously hard to prove how accurate our dreams are. As we've already seen, we dream in images, and their importance, and how we define those images is inevitably a subjective exercise. We bring our own experience to the dream and our understanding reflects that experience. Added to this, as many experts readily acknowledge, we may also dream symbolically. So, the images that we view in our dreams may actually represent people or places in our life as well as relationships and our perceptions of events. Consequently, dream interpretation can't but help be an inexact science.

That said, scientists have attempted to explain away the phenomenon and most theories conclude that precognitive dreams are simply the result of chance or coincidence. In other words, if you involve enough people in a survey – and generally research into something like precognitive dreams relies on members of the general public who choose to contribute – then the law of averages ensures that someone, somewhere, will give you the answer that you're looking for.

One expert even likens the whole business to winning the pools. We all know that there's something like a million to one chance of us scooping the big prize, but the truth is, because of the huge amounts of people who do the pools every week, someone has to win. And for many scientists, the same logic applies to someone dreaming of an event that actually does tell the future – someone has got to get it right at some stage.

Could your dream predict the future?

Precognitive dreamers note that the dreams that foretell the future are significantly different from 'ordinary' dreams. They are always more vivid than usual and often much more intense. The content of the dream may initially be surprising – pleasantly or otherwise – although the images and 'story' it tells may be more meaningful than other dreams where associations can be disjointed and illogical. People have also remarked that such dreams have a tremendous impact on them, much more so than normal, and cause the dreamer to wake up, determined to act upon it. The action could involve something as insignificant as making a phone call or something major like reorganising a journey to avoid the place where an accident takes place in a dream.

If you do feel that some of your dreams are precognitive, make a point of jotting them down in your dream diary. Pay attention to all the details that you can remember and be sure to date it. That way you will have a foolproof record if, or when, something happens that you have already dream of.

Don't feel embarrassed to follow up the dreams; if you dreamt that Uncle Sid was ill, a phone call to ask generally how he is doing certainly wouldn't go amiss. If fact, even if he's fine, he'll probably still appreciate your interest! Check the papers to see if you can find any connections there and talk to friends and relatives so you can get a wider picture of what's been happening – locally as well as nationally.

Most important, if you do discover that your dreams predict the future then be assured that you are not alone. Thousands of people share this ability. What's more, if events have proved that your premonitions are right then you will know that you should regard a dream of this kind as a warning. Take heed if you possibly can. It is surely much better to rearrange something than to regret the fact that you did nothing at all. And if someone else tells you that they've had what they feel is a dream of the future, don't simply dismiss it as fanciful. Remember, there's an awful lot that happens that is far stranger than truth.

Smoking

The Dream

You find yourself at a party or in some other sociable setting, when all of a sudden, you notice you have a lighted cigarette in your hand – without the slightest understanding of how it got there.

The Meaning

How you react to this scenario and what it means for you will depend partly on whether you are a smoker in everyday life. Today, it's difficult for even the most hardened smoker not to feel a faint tinge of guilt at the very least about indulging in such an antisocial and unhealthy habit. Yet even people who have never smoked report having this kind of dream sometimes, and almost always associate it with feelings of anxiety or guilt. Young people in particular find themselves being 'caught' smoking by an adult who disapproves, such as a parent or teacher.

Several sleep researchers have themselves written of smoking dreams which they interpreted without too much difficulty. One of them had given up the habit three weeks before he started having recurring dreams in which he was horrified to find himself with a group of friends, enjoying a cigarette. Furious with himself, he stamped it out, and woke overwhelmed with feelings of guilt and anxiety. Although the content of the dream changed with time, he was shocked at the depth of addiction which these dreams revealed, although they did meet Freud's description of dreams as satisfying a fundamental drive – in this case oral satisfaction.

Another researcher saw quite clearly in a dream an X-ray of his own lung showing the presence of cancer, and was told by a doctor who examined him that it had spread to other parts of his body. His feelings of shock and regret at not having given up before it was too late were so profound that as soon as he woke up, he decided to stop smoking.

Making the dream work for you

If you, too, are an ex-smoker, like the researcher whose story is recounted above, you can simply take your dream as a recognition of the power of the addiction you are trying to overcome. It's probably that feelings of shame, guilt and failure were part and parcel of your dream, so it's a good idea to hang on to the memory of how you felt when you thought you'd taken up smoking again. Then if you're ever tempted to backslide, remind yourself of how bad you'd feel if you really did weaken. It may take a year or two for the dreams to fade altogether, but in the meantime you can use them to reinforce your will-power.

Smokers will probably find that guilt is a feature of any smoking dreams they experience too. Most people know, however they try to ignore it, that smoking is bad for their own health and increases their susceptibility to all kinds of illness. Not only that, it can affect others who share the same home or workplace, as well as being increasingly frowned upon by public opinion. So your dream may be related to buried feelings about your own habit which could be brought into the open to help you make a decision to give up. Alternatively, a smoking dream may reflect guilty feelings about some other aspect of your life, with smoking simply acting as a symbol for the thing that's really bothering you. If you think this could be the explanation in your case, ask yourself:

- Is there some aspect of your life which needs sorting out?

- Do you have a guilty conscience about something you've said or done?

- Are you carrying or in a job, or with a relationship, which is less than satisfactory?

Action
Once you've decided whether your dream is really about some aspect of smoking or just a cover for something else, you can work out what exactly is going on. When it's a question of breaking yourself of an addiction which you know is harming you – and possibly others too – it's up to you how you decide to deal with it. There are many sources of advice and support. Start by talking to your doctor who can, if necessary, give you advice about aids to giving up, like nicotine patches or gum, and refer to other sources of information and help.

Otherwise, your next step will depend on exactly what you feel is wrong, but basically you need to face up to whatever is making you feel guilty and see what you can do to change things. An unsatisfactory relationship or job can't be changed overnight, but at least you can talk to other people concerned – your partner, your boss and/or your colleagues and make it clear that things aren't right.

A *day in your life* . . .

The events and people that inhabit our dream world can, as we've seen, be literally whatever we want them to be. In a way, that's what makes dreams and dreaming so fascinating. We get to play casting director, producer and designer as well as taking the star role! Of course most dreams can be linked back to our own personal experiences, which is why much of them consist of images and events that reflect our wishes, worries, hopes and expectations.

The images that our dreams use to depict these feelings are often linked to events that have happened to us, directly or indirectly, during the previous day. So, if you're addicted to *Neighbours* on television, you shouldn't necessarily be surprised if at some point an Australian setting pops up in one of your dreams!

But, however much attention and thought you pay to your dream world there are times when our night-time images defy meaning. Maybe what you're seeing is a result of your brain filtering all the minutiae that have gathered throughout the day, or perhaps it's a visual example of how your mind sorts out what's happened, putting it into order so that you're able to deal with all the 'material' effectively during your waking world.

Whatever the explanation, what's interesting is that there are several recurring – and seemingly nonsensical – themes that, while they only affect a small group of people, are sufficiently common to justify a mention in a dream book such as this.

Teeth

One often-quoted dream is about teeth. Dreamers report 'seeing' their teeth fall out: sometimes it's a clean break, happening in one fell swoop, at other times people feel their teeth breaking into bits, and the only way the dreamer can get rid of them is to spit them out. Experts vary in their explanation, although current theories range from a fear of ageing to fear of change.

No one has yet suggested that there may be a link between the state of one's teeth and the narrative depicted in such a dream, and if you are predisposed to such dreams and are also concerned about your dental health, a visit to the dentist might not go amiss!

Lifts

It's rather odd, but it does seem that lifts figure in dreams more often than one might expect. However, it is not the lift itself that commentators think is important but rather its symbolic implications. In other words, a dreamer who is inside one could be seen as 'moving up' in the world. If you were to dream of yourself on an escalator, or even climbing a tree, the meaning may very well be the same. The obvious conclusion to be drawn from this is that if you see yourself going up then this could suggest that you are about to wing your way towards great heights and that you should try not to let anything stand in your way. Equally, if your dream shows you going in a downward direction, you may not see your life in quite such a positive way.

Celebrities

The last but equally significant dream with a theme concerns those which depict celebrities. You may, inexplicably, find yourself surrounded by a host of stars, with you as the only person without an obvious claim to fame. Alternatively, you could be doing something perfectly normal (anything from shopping to eating supper), although your companion just happens to be a Hollywood superstar!

As with dreams of royalty, film stars and celebrities can represent significant figures in your life. Maybe you feel someone is trying to lead you astray? Or you worry that your pursuit of a good time could result in disastrous long-term problems? Stars may reflect the more frivolous side of your character or they may represent a world that you're desperate to join. Maybe you even have an unconscious desire to be part of the Hollywood jet set in an attempt to break out of what you consider is a humdrum existence. For some, the celebrity world is the ultimate fantasy. On a superficial level (and let's face it, that is the way that it is generally conveyed through newspapers and magazines) stardom means status, excitement, passion and freedom from financial, and even family, ties.

So, if stardom does figure in your dreams, you could do a lot worse than enjoy the fantasy for what it is. Just be sure not to confuse it with reality because, however hard it may be to believe from where you're sitting, the stars really do have their problems too.

conclusions

We hope that after reading this book, you will look forward to bedtime in quite a new way. Instead of just 'closing down' for the night, you can anticipate entering a whole new world of experience, entertainment and even understanding. If you have always been the kind of person who claimed not to dream at all or only remembered your dreams on rare occasions, you now know that in reality you will be spending quite a large part of each night in fantasy land.

To make the most of this new insight, your next step must be to train yourself to remember your dreams or remember more of them at least – until you can do that, you can't start to benefit from the insight they can give you into your everyday life. Sadly, you probably won't get any stunning overnight revelations about how to change your life – interpreting your dreams doesn't work like that. In fact, the more effort and thought you put into extracting meaning, the more worthwhile the result is likely to be. In the end, there's still a lot we don't know about our dreams – why we dream and what it all means. The good news is that this means no one can tell you that your own conclusions are wrong. Dream interpretation is an inexact, and very personal, art and once you get into it, it's enormous fun too!

further reading

Brenda Mallon, *Children Dreaming*, Penguin, 1989.

Christopher Evans and Peter Evans, *Landscapes of the Night: How and why we dream*, Gollancz, 1983.

Gay Gaer Luce and Julius Segal, *Sleep*, Coward, McCann, Geoghegan Inc., New York, 1966.

Jacob Empson, *Sleep and Dreaming*, Harvester Wheatsheaf.

Dr Keith Hearne, *The Dream Machine*, by post from 35 Robyn's Way, Sevenoaks, Kent, TN13 3EB.

Dr Jim Horne, *Why We Sleep*, OUP.

Patricia Garfield, *Women's Bodies, Women's Dreams*, Ballantine Books, New York, 1988.